Basic Understanding of Financial Investment

I0464414

Book 6

For Teens and Young Adults

By Ronald E. Hudkins

Description

It doesn't matter if you are a complete investing novice or simply abundantly confused about all the contradictory financial advice you are inundated with, this basic guide to Investing is an accessible guide. This book is your introduction to understanding financial investment and is one of the most important books you will ever read on how to understand the available financial tools, instruments and applications.

Investing (like many things) is all about common sense. This book should be in every career counselor's office and delivered to every teen or young adult as it contains savvy financial advice for today's street-smart young investors. It is filled with in-depth insights and practical basic advice. The financial lingo and clear explanations allow this book to be easily digested by a novice

Wouldn't it be great if someone could really explain to you-in plain and simple English-the basics that must be known about investing in order to insure your financial success? This excellent practical personal finance guide really shows young investors the tools available to them to achieve financial freedom. It is an extraordinary and timely book offering guidance every beginning investor needs to understand.

With this book you will understand how to invest in a sensible, low-cost and effective manner with or without the assistance of an advisor. It gives you the basics of getting started and the motivation to handle your own money. It will give you the building blocks to create a solid investment portfolio that, over the course of a lifetime will make you wealthy.

Financial Disclaimer

The Content is intended only as a base reference to help you make financial decisions. It is broad in scope and does not consider your personal financial situation. Your personal financial situation is unique and the information and advice may not be appropriate for your situation. Accordingly, before making any final decisions or implementing any financial strategy, I recommend that you obtain additional information and advice of your accountant and other financial advisors who are fully aware of your individual circumstances.

You are advised to undertake your Due diligence by investigating any business or person prior to signing a contract.

You should consider this your legal obligation and as such apply it to your voluntary investigations. A common example of due diligence in various industries is the process through which a potential acquirer evaluates a target company or its assets before an acquisition. The theory behind due diligence thus holds that performing this type of investigation contributes significantly to informed decision making by enhancing the amount and quality of information available to you the decision maker. You should ensure that the information gathered is systematically used to deliberate in a reflexive manner on the decision(s) at hand and all information factors in the costs, benefits, and risks you anticipate to undertake.

DEDICATION

I dedicate this book to teens and young adults looking for sound advice on how to make smart financial choices needed to establish a firm footing as you work your way through school and the post-graduation years.

Just remember as your speeding down that new found road of freedom that how you spend your 20's financially will ultimately define you.

After all is said and done you should also know; after you get married, someone should know how to write a check correctly, save and invest. Because, even if you have tons of love, there's still going to be a lot of bills!

Table of Contents

Title Page

Copyright

Description

Financial Disclaimer

Dedication

Introduction - Why Invest?

Chapter One

Chapter Two – Investment Products

Introduction - Why Invest?

A few people may stumble into financial security. But for most people, the only way to attain financial security is to save and invest over a long period of time. You just need to have your money work for you. That's investing.

There are two ways your money can work for you:

- **Your money earns money.** Someone pays you to use your money for a period of time. You then get your money back plus "interest." Or, if you buy stock in a company that pays "dividends" to shareholders, the company pays you a portion of its earnings on a regular basis. Now your money is making an "income."

- **You buy something with your money that could increase in value.** You become an owner of something that you hope increases in value over time. When you need your money back, you sell it, hoping someone else will pay you more for it.

Compound interest is a key aspect of investing. With compound interest, you earn interest on the money you save and on the interest that money earns. Over time, even a small amount of savings can add up to big money and help you achieve your financial goals.

Sweet: If you buy a $1 candy bar every day, it adds up to $365 a year. Put that $365 into an investment that earns 5% a year, and it would grow to $465.84 by the end of five years. By the end of 30 years, you would have $1,577.50. That's the power of "compounding."

All investments involve some degree of risk. If you intend to purchase securities such as stocks, bonds, or mutual funds, it's important that you understand before you invest that you could lose some or all of your money.

Unlike deposits at FDIC-insured banks and NCUA-insured credit unions, the money you invest in securities is not federally insured. You could lose your principal, which is the amount you've invested. That's true even if you purchase the securities through a bank.

The reward for taking on risk is the potential for a greater investment return. If you have a financial goal with a long-term horizon, you may make more money by carefully investing in higher-risk assets, such as stocks or bonds. On the other hand, investing solely in cash investments may be appropriate for short-term financial goals. The principal concern for individuals investing in cash equivalents is inflation risk, which is the risk that inflation will outpace and erode returns.

[i]http://investor.gov/introduction-markets/why-invest

Chapter One

Five Questions to Ask Before You Invest

Whether you're a first-time investor or have been investing for many years, there are some basic questions you should always ask before you commit your hard-earned money to an investment.

Question 1: Is the seller licensed?

Research shows that con-artists are experts at the art of persuasion, often using a variety of influence tactics tailored to the vulnerabilities of their victims. Smart investors check the background of anyone promoting an investment opportunity, even before learning about opportunity itself.

- *Researching brokers*: Details on a broker's background and qualifications are available for free on FINRA's BrokerCheck website.

- *Researching investment advisers*: The Investment Adviser Public Disclosure website provides information about investment adviser firms registered with the SEC and most state-registered investment adviser firms.

If you are not sure who to contact or have any questions regarding checking the background of an investment professional, call the SEC's toll-free investor assistance line at (800) 732-0330.

Question 2: Is the investment registered?

Any offer or sale of securities must be registered with the SEC or exempt from registration. Registration is important because it provides investors with access to key information about the company's management, products, services, and finances.

Smart investors always check whether an investment is registered with the SEC by using the SEC's EDGAR database or contacting the SEC's toll-free investor assistance line at (800) 732-0330.

Question 3: How do the risks compare with the potential rewards?

The potential for greater returns comes with greater risk. Understanding this crucial trade-off between risk and reward can help you separate legitimate opportunities from unlawful schemes.

Investments with greater risk may offer higher potential returns, but they may expose you to greater investment losses. Keep in mind every investment carries some degree of risk and no legitimate investment offers the best of both worlds.

Many investment frauds are pitched as high return opportunities with little or no risk. Ignore these so-called opportunities or, better yet, report them to the SEC.

Question 4: Do you understand the investment?

Many successful investors follow this rule of thumb: *Never invest in something you don't understand*. Be sure to always read an investment's prospectus or disclosure statement carefully. If you can't understand the investment and how it will help you make money, ask a trusted financial professional for help. If you are still confused, you should think twice about investing.

Question 5: Where can you turn for help?

Whether checking out an investment professional, researching an investment, or learning about new products or scams, unbiased information can be a great advantage when it comes to investing wisely. Make a habit of using the information and tools on securities regulators' websites. If you have a question or concern about an investment, please contact the SEC, FINRA, or your state securities regulator for help.

ⁱⁱhttp://investor.gov/investing-basics/guiding-principles/five-questions-ask-before-you-invest

Investing on Your Own

The first step to investing, especially investing on your own, is to make sure you have a financial plan. How much are you going to invest? For how long? What are your financial goals? Do you understand your tolerance for risk? All investments carry some risk.

The next step is research, research, research. When investing on your own, you are responsible for your decisions. How will you select one stock, bond, or mutual fund over others? Always make sure that all securities are registered with the SEC, using the SEC's EDGAR database. Don't purchase solely on stock tips from others.

There are several ways you can invest on your own, including Online Investing, Direct Investing, and Dividend Reinvestment Plans.

What do you know about saving and investing? Do you want to see how your financial knowledge measures up against others? Try the Investor.gov quizzes.

http://investor.gov/researching-managing-investments/investing-your-own

Online Investing

Online trading is quick and easy, but online investing takes time.

With the click of a mouse, you can buy and sell stocks from one of the many online brokers offering low-cost trades. Although online trading saves investors time and money, it does not take the homework out of making investment decisions. You may be able to make a fast trade, but making wise investment decisions takes time. Before you trade, know why you are buying or selling, and the risk of your investment.

Set your price limits

If you place an order, check to make sure it was executed

If you cancel an order, make sure the cancellation worked before placing another trade

If you purchase a security in a cash account, you must pay for it before you can sell it.

Set your price limits

To avoid buying or selling a stock at a price higher or lower than you wanted, you should place a limit order rather than a market order.

A limit order is an order to buy or sell a security at a specific price. A buy limit order can only be executed at the limit price or lower, and a sell limit order can only be executed at the limit price or higher. Your limit order will not be executed if the market price quickly surpasses your limit before your order can be filled. But, by using a limit order, you protect yourself from buying the stock at too high a price or selling it at too low a price.

If you place an order, check to make sure it was executed

Some investors mistakenly assume that their orders have not been executed and place the order again. They end up buying or selling twice, which can be a costly mistake. Talk with your financial services firm about how you should handle a situation where you are unsure if your original order was executed.

If you cancel an order, make sure the cancellation worked before placing another trade

When you cancel an online trade, make sure that your original transaction was not executed. Although you may receive an electronic receipt for the cancellation, don't assume the trade was cancelled. Orders can only be cancelled if they have not been executed. Ask your financial services firm about how you can confirm that a cancellation order worked.

If you purchase a security in a cash account, you must pay for it before you can sell it

In a cash account, you must pay for the purchase of a stock before you sell it. If you buy and sell a stock before paying for it, you are freeriding. Freeriding violates the credit extension provisions of the Federal Reserve Board's Regulation T. If you freeride, your broker must "freeze" your account for 90 days. You can still trade but you must pay in full for any purchases on the date you buy them as long as the freeze is in effect.

You can avoid the freeze if you pay for the stock in full by the settlement date, using funds that do not come from the sale of the stock. You can always ask your broker for an extension or waiver, but you may not get it.

http://investor.gov/researching-managing-investments/investing-your-own/online-investing

Direct Investing

You may be able to invest directly using direct stock plans (DSP) or dividend reinvestment plans (DRIP). Here's how they work:

Direct stock plans (DSP). Some companies allow you to buy or sell their stock directly through them without using a broker. This saves on commissions, but you may have to pay other fees to the plan, such as fees incurred if you transfer shares to a broker to sell them. Some companies limit direct stock plans to employees of the company or existing shareholders. Some require minimum amounts for purchases or account levels. You'll want to read and understand the plan's rules before investing.

Direct stock plans usually will not allow you to buy or sell shares at a specific market price or at a specific time. Instead, the company will buy or sell shares for the plan at set times — such as daily, weekly, or monthly — and at an average market price. Depending on the plan, you may be able to automate your purchases and have the cost deducted automatically from your savings account.

Dividend reinvestment plans (DRIP). These plans allow you to buy more shares of a stock you already own by reinvesting dividend payments into the company. You must sign an agreement with the company to have this done. Check with the company or your brokerage firm to see if you will be charged for this service.

[iii]http://investor.gov/researching-managing-investments/investing-your-own/direct-investing

Researching Investments

Researching investments is part of an investor's due diligence. Companies must provide certain information when they initially offer stocks or bonds for sale to the public. Companies and bond issuers must also must provide certain information to the public periodically. These disclosures provide investors with information to judge whether a particular security is a good investment. If a company is not registered with the SEC, or a bond issuer is not registered with the Municipal Securities Rulemaking Board (MSRB), it could be a red flag. Scams often involve unregistered companies.

Ask and Check - Research Investment Products and Professionals

Using EDGAR - Researching Public Companies

Using EMMA - Researching Municipal Securities and 529 Plans

How to Read a 10-K

How to Read an 8-K

Insider Transactions and Forms 3, 4, and 5

Chapter Two – Investment Products

While the author nor the SEC cannot recommend any particular investment, you should know that a vast array of investment products exists – including stocks and stock mutual funds, bonds and bond mutual funds, lifecycle funds, exchange-traded funds, certificates of deposit, money market funds, and annuities.

This section describes some of these investment products, explains how they are bought and sold, and details their benefits and risks. You'll also find information on fees and tips to avoid fraud.

Please use the menu to the left to learn more information about each of the products.

[iv]http://investor.gov/investing-basics/investment-products

Section 1

Saving for Education - 529 Plans

What is a 529 plan?

A 529 plan is a tax-advantaged savings plan designed to encourage saving for future college costs. These plans, legally known as "qualified tuition plans," are sponsored by states, state agencies, or educational institutions, and are authorized by Section 529 of the Internal Revenue Code.

Two types of 529 plans -- prepaid tuition and college savings:

There are two types of 529 plans: pre-paid tuition plans and college savings plans. All 50 states and the District of Columbia sponsor at least one type of 529 plan. In addition, a group of private colleges and universities sponsor a pre-paid tuition plan.

Summary of Topics Covered:

a. What are the differences between pre-paid tuition plans and college savings plans?

b. How does investing in a 529 plan affect federal and state income taxes?

c. Does investing in a 529 plan impact financial aid eligibility?

d. What fees and expenses will I pay if I invest in a 529 plan?

e. Is there any way to purchase a 529 plan but avoid some of the extra fees?

f. What questions should I ask before I invest in a 529 plan?

g. Where can I find more information?

h. Other Online Resources

a. What are the differences between pre-paid tuition plans and college savings plans?

- **Pre-paid tuition plans** generally allow college savers to purchase units or credits at participating colleges and universities for future tuition and, in some cases, room and board. Most prepaid tuition plans are sponsored by state governments and have residency requirements. Many state governments guarantee investments in pre-paid tuition plans that they sponsor.

- **College savings plans** generally permit a college saver, also called the "account holder," to establish an account for a student (the "beneficiary") for the purpose of paying for the beneficiary's eligible college expenses.

- An account holder may typically choose among several investment options which often include stock mutual funds, bond mutual funds, and money market funds, as well as age-based portfolios that automatically shift toward a more conservative mix of investments as the beneficiary gets closer to college age.

- Withdrawals from college savings plans generally can be used at any college or university. Investments in college savings plans that invest in mutual funds are not guaranteed by state governments and are not federally insured.

The chart below shows some of the major differences between pre-paid tuition plans and college savings plans:

Prepaid Tuition Plan	College Savings Plan
Locks in tuition prices at eligible public and private colleges and universities.	No lock on college costs.
All plans cover tuition and mandatory fees only. Some plans allow you to purchase a room & board option or use excess tuition credits for other qualified expenses.	Covers all "qualified higher education expenses," including: tuition, room & board, mandatory fees, books, and computers (if required).
Most plans set lump sum and installment payments prior to purchase based on age of beneficiary and number of years of college tuition purchased.	No state guarantee. Most investment options are subject to market risk. Your investment may make no profit or even decline in value.

Most plans have age/grade limit for beneficiary.	No age limits. Open to adults and children.
Most state plans require either owner or beneficiary of plan to be a state resident.	No residency requirement. However, nonresidents may only be able to purchase some plans through financial advisers or brokers.
Most plans have limited enrollment period.	Enrollment open all year.

Source: Smart Saving for College, FINRA®

b. How does investing in a 529 plan affect federal and state income taxes?

- Investing in a 529 plan may offer college savers special tax benefits. Earnings in 529 plans are not subject to federal tax, and in most cases, state tax, provided you use withdrawals for eligible college expenses, such as tuition and room and board.

- However, if you withdraw money from a 529 plan and do not use it for an eligible college expense, you generally will be subject to income tax and a 10% federal tax penalty on earnings. Many states offer state income tax or other benefits, such as matching grants, for investing in a 529 plan. But you may only be eligible for these benefits if you participate in a 529 plan sponsored by your state of residence. Just a few states allow residents to deduct contributions to any 529 plan from state income tax returns.

c. Does investing in a 529 plan impact financial aid eligibility?

Investing in a 529 plan generally will reduce a student's eligibility to participate in need-based financial aid. Assets held in pre-paid tuition plans and college savings plans have been treated similarly for federal financial aid purposes since mid-2006. Both are treated as parental assets when calculating the expected family contribution toward college costs.

d. What fees and expenses will I pay if I invest in a 529 plan?

- It is important to understand the fees and expenses associated with 529 plans because they lower your returns. Fees and expenses will vary based on the type of plan. Prepaid tuition plans typically charge enrollment and administrative fees. In addition to "loads" for broker-sold plans, college savings plans may charge enrollment fees, annual maintenance fees, and asset management fees.

- Some of these fees are collected by the state sponsor of the plan, and some are collected by the financial services firms hired by the state sponsor to manage the 529 program. Some college savings plans will waive or reduce some of these fees if you maintain a large account balance, participate in an automatic contribution plan, or are a resident of the state sponsoring the 529 plan.

e. Is there any way to purchase a 529 plan but avoid some of the extra fees?

Direct-Sold College Savings Plans. States offer college savings plans that residents and, in many cases, non-residents can invest in without paying a "load," or sales fee. This type of plan, which you can buy directly from the plan's sponsor or program manager without the assistance of a broker, is generally less expensive because it waives or does not charge sales fees that may apply to broker-sold plans. For information, contact the plan's sponsor or program manager or visit the plan's website. Websites such as the one maintained by the College Savings Plan Network, as well as a number of commercial websites, provide links to most 529 plan websites.

f. What questions should I ask before I invest in a 529 plan?

- Is the plan available directly from the state or plan sponsor?

- Does the plan offer special benefits for state residents? Would I be better off investing in my state's plan or another plan? Does my state's plan offer tax advantages or other benefits for investment in the plan it sponsors? If my state's plan charges higher fees than another state's plan, do the tax advantages or other benefits offered by my state outweigh the benefit of investing in another state's less expensive plan?

- What fees are charged by the plan? How much of my investment goes to compensating a broker? Under what circumstances does the plan waive or reduce certain fees?

- What are the plan's withdrawal restrictions? Which colleges and universities participate in the plan? What types of college expenses are covered by the plan?

- What types of investment options are offered by the plan? How long are contributions held before being invested?

- What limitations apply to the plan? When can an account holder change investment options, switch beneficiaries, or transfer ownership of the account to another account holder?

- Who is the program manager? How has the plan performed in the past?

g. Where can I find more information?

Offering Circulars

Often called a "disclosure statement," "disclosure document," or "program description," the offering circular for a 529 plan will have detailed information about the plan, including investment options, tax benefits and consequences, fees and expenses, financial aid questions, limitations, and risks. Most 529 plans post their offering circulars online. The National Association of State Treasurers created the College Savings Plan Network, which provides links to most 529 plan websites.

h. Other Online Resources

- You can learn more about 529 plans and other college saving options on FINRA's Smart Saving for College website. The website contains links to other sites, including the College Savings Plan Network. Also, see FINRA's investor alert on 529 plans.

- Additional information is available in the Internal Revenue Service's Publication 970 (Tax Benefits for Higher Education).

- Use EMMA - Researching Municipal Securities and 529 Plans

[v]http://investor.gov/investing-basics/investment-products/saving-your-childs-education-529-plans

Section 2 - Annuities

What are annuities?

An annuity is a contract between you and an insurance company that requires the insurer to make payments to you, either immediately or in the future. You buy an annuity by making either a single payment or a series of payments. Similarly, your payout may come either as one lump-sum payment or as a series of payments over time.

a. Why do people buy annuities?
b. What kinds of annuities are there?
c. What are the benefits and risks of variable annuities?
d. How to buy and sell annuities
e. Understanding fees
f. Avoiding fraud
g. Additional information

a. Why do people buy annuities?

People typically buy annuities to help manage their income in retirement. Annuities provide three things:

- **Periodic payments for a specific amount of time.** This may be for the rest of your life, or the life of your spouse or another person.

- **Death benefits.** If you die before you start receiving payments, the person you name as your beneficiary receives a specific payment.

- **Tax-deferred growth.** You pay no taxes on the income and investment gains from your annuity until you withdraw the money.

b. What kinds of annuities are there?

There are three basic types of annuities, fixed, variable and indexed. Here is how they work:

- **Fixed annuity.** The insurance company promises you a minimum rate of interest and a fixed amount of periodic payments. Fixed annuities are regulated by state insurance commissioners. Please check with your state insurance commission about the risks and benefits of fixed annuities and to confirm that your insurance broker is registered to sell insurance in your state.

- **Variable annuity.** The insurance company allows you to direct your annuity payments to different investment options, usually mutual funds. Your payout will vary depending on how much you put in, the rate of return on your investments, and expenses. The SEC regulates variable annuities.

- **Indexed annuity.** This annuity combines features of securities and insurance products. The insurance company credits you with a return that is based on a stock market index, such as the Standard & Poor's 500 Index. Indexed annuities are regulated by state insurance commissioners.

c. What are the benefits and risks of variable annuities?

Some people look to annuities to "insure" their retirement and to receive periodic payments once they no longer receive a salary. There are two phases to annuities, the accumulation phase and the payout phase.

- During the accumulation phase, you make payments that may be split among various investment options. In addition, variable annuities often allow you to put some of your money in an account that pays a fixed rate of interest.

- During the payout phase, you get your payments back, along with any investment income and gains. You may take the payout in one lump-sum payment, or you may choose to receive a regular stream of payments, generally monthly.

All investments carry a level of risk. Make sure you consider the financial strength of the insurance company issuing the annuity. You want to be sure the company will still be around, and financially sound, during your payout phase.

Variable annuities have a number of features that you need to understand before you invest. Understand that variable annuities are designed as an investment for long-term goals, such as retirement. They are not suitable for short-term goals because you typically will pay substantial taxes and charges or other penalties if you withdraw your money early. Variable annuities also involve investment risks, just as mutual funds do.

d. How to buy and sell annuities

Insurance companies sell annuities, as do some banks, brokerage firms, and mutual fund companies. Make sure you read and understand your annuity contract. All fees should be clearly stated in the contract. Your most important source of information about investment options within a variable annuity is the mutual fund prospectus. Request prospectuses for all the mutual fund options you might want to select. Read the prospectuses carefully before you decide how to allocate your purchase payments among the investment options.

Realize that if you are investing in a variable annuity through a tax-advantaged retirement plan, such as a 401(k) plan or an Individual Retirement Account, you will get no additional tax advantages from a variable annuity. In such cases, consider buying a variable annuity only if it makes sense because of the annuity's other features.

Note that if you sell or withdraw money from a variable annuity too soon after your purchase, the insurance company will impose a "surrender charge." This is a type of sales charge that applies in the "surrender period," typically six to eight years after you buy the annuity. Surrender charges will reduce the value of -- and the return on -- your investment.

e. Understanding fees

You will pay several charges when you invest in a variable annuity. Be sure you understand all charges before you invest. Besides surrender charges, there are a number of other charges, including:

- **Mortality and expense risk charge**. This charge is equal to a certain percentage of your account value, typically about 1.25% per year. This charge pays the issuer for the insurance risk it assumes under the annuity contract. The profit from this charge sometimes is used to pay a commission to the person who sold you the annuity.

- **Administrative fees.** The issuer may charge you for record keeping and other administrative expenses. This may be a flat annual fee, or a percentage of your account value.

- **Underlying fund expenses**. In addition to fees charged by the issuer, you will pay the fees and expenses for underlying mutual fund investments.

- **Fees and charges for other features.** Additional fees typically apply for special features, such as a guaranteed minimum income benefit or long-term care insurance. Initial sales loads, fees for transferring part of your account from one investment option to another, and other fees also may apply.

- **Penalties.** If you withdraw money from an annuity before you are age 59 ½, you may have to pay a 10% tax penalty to the Internal Revenue Service on top of any taxes you owe on the income.

f. Avoiding fraud

Variable annuities are considered to be securities. All broker-dealers and investment advisers that sell variable annuities must be registered. Before buying an annuity from a broker or adviser, confirm that they are registered using BrokerCheck.

In most cases, the investments offered within a variable annuity are mutual funds. By law, each mutual fund is required to file a prospectus and regular shareholder reports with the SEC. Before you invest, be sure to read these materials.

g. Additional information

Annuities
Variable Annuities - What You Should Know
Investor Bulletin: Indexed Annuities
Investor Bulletin: Variable Annuities

Section 3 - Bonds

What are bonds?

A bond is a debt security, similar to an IOU. Borrowers issue bonds to raise money from investors willing to lend them money for a certain amount of time.

When you buy a bond, you are lending to the issuer, which may be a government, municipality, or corporation. In return, the issuer promises to pay you a specified rate of interest during the life of the bond and to repay the principal, also known as face value or par value of the bond, when it "matures," or comes due after a set period of time.

Summary of Topics Covered:

a. Why do people buy bonds?
b. What types of bonds are there?
c. What are the benefits and risks of bonds?
d. Avoiding fraud
e. Additional information

a. Why do people buy bonds?

Investors buy bonds because:

- They provide a predictable income stream. Typically, bonds pay interest twice a year.

- If the bonds are held to maturity, bondholders get back the entire principal, so bonds are a way to preserve capital while investing.

- Bonds can help offset exposure to more volatile stock holdings.

Companies, governments and municipalities issue bonds to get money for various things, which may include:

- Providing operating cash flow

- Financing debt

- Funding capital investments in schools, highways, hospitals, and other projects

b. What types of bonds are there?

There are three main types of bonds:

- **Corporate bonds** are debt securities issued by private and public corporations.

- **Investment-grade.** These bonds have a higher credit rating, implying less credit risk, than high-yield corporate bonds.

- **High-yield**. These bonds have a lower credit rating, implying higher credit risk, than investment-grade bonds and, therefore, offer higher interest rates in return for the increased risk.

- **Municipal bonds**, called "Munis," are debt securities issued by states, cities, counties and other government entities. Types of "Munis" include:

- **General obligation bonds**. These bonds are not secured by any assets; instead, they are backed by the "full faith and credit" of the issuer, which has the power to tax residents to pay bondholders.

- **Revenue bonds.** Instead of taxes, these bonds are backed by revenues from a specific project or source, such as highway tolls or lease fees. Some revenue bonds are "non-recourse," meaning that if the revenue stream dries up, the bondholders do not have a claim on the underlying revenue source.

- **Conduit bonds.** Governments sometimes issue municipal bonds on behalf of private entities such as non-profit colleges or hospitals. These "conduit" borrowers typically agree to repay the issuer, who pays the interest and principal on the bonds. If the conduit borrower fails to make a payment, the issuer usually is not required to pay the bondholders.

- **U.S. Treasuries** are issued by the U.S. Department of the Treasury on behalf of the federal government. They carry the full faith and credit of the U.S. government, making them a safe and popular investment. Types of U.S. Treasury debt include:

- **Treasury Bills**. Short-term securities maturing in a few days to 52 weeks

- **Notes.** Longer-term securities maturing within ten years

- **Bonds.** Long-term securities that typically mature in 30 years and pay interest every six months

- **TIPS.** Treasury Inflation-Protected Securities are notes and bonds whose principal is adjusted based on changes in the Consumer Price Index. TIPS pay interest every six months and are issued with maturities of five, ten, and 30 years.

c. What are the benefits and risks of bonds?

Bonds can provide a means of preserving capital and earning a predictable return. Bond investments provide steady streams of income from interest payments prior to maturity.

The interest from municipal bonds generally is exempt from federal income tax and also may be exempt from state and local taxes for residents in the states where the bond is issued.

As with any investment, bonds have risks. These risks include:

Credit risk. The issuer may fail to timely make interest or principal payments and thus default on its bonds.

Interest rate risk. Interest rate changes can affect a bond's value. If bonds are held to maturity the investor will receive the face value, plus interest. If sold before maturity, the bond may be worth more or less than the face value. Rising interest rates will make newly issued bonds more appealing to investors because the newer bonds will have a higher rate of interest than older ones. To sell an older bond with a lower interest rate, you might have to sell it at a discount.

Inflation risk. Inflation is a general upward movement in prices. Inflation reduces purchasing power, which is a risk for investors receiving a fixed rate of interest.

Liquidity risk. This refers to the risk that investors won't find a market for the bond, potentially preventing them from buying or selling when they want.

Call risk. The possibility that a bond issuer retires a bond before its maturity date, something an issuer might do if interest rates decline, much like a homeowner might refinance a mortgage to benefit from lower interest rates.

d. Avoiding fraud

Corporate bonds are securities and, if publicly offered, must be registered with the SEC. The registration of these securities can be verified using the SEC's EDGAR system. Be wary of any person who attempts to sell non-registered bonds.

Most municipal securities issued after July 3, 1995 are required to file annual financial information, operating data, and notices of certain events with the Municipal Securities Rulemaking Board (MSRB). This information is available free of charge online at www.emma.msrb.org. If the municipal bond is not filed with MSRB, this could be a red flag.

e. Additional information

Investor Bulletin: What are Corporate Bonds
Investor Bulletin: What are High-yield Corporate Bonds
Investor Bulletin: Interest Rate Risk
MSRB Investor Guide 2012
Bond Funds and Income Funds
Callable or Redeemable Bonds
Financial Industry Regulatory Authority (FINRA)
Information on CUSIP numbers

Late Payment of Interest on Bonds
Municipal Securities Rulemaking Board (MSRB)
MSRB Electronic Municipal Market Access
(EMMA)
The Securities Industry and Financial Markets
Association (SIFMA)

http://investor.gov/investing-
basics/investment-products/bonds [vii]

Section 4 - Certificates of Deposit (CDs)

What are certificates of deposit?

A certificate of deposit (CD) is a savings account that holds a fixed amount of money for a fixed period of time, such as six months, one year, or five years, and in exchange, the issuing bank pays interest. When you cash in or redeem your CD, you receive the money you originally invested plus any interest. Certificates of deposit are considered to be one of the safest savings options. A CD bought through a federally insured bank is insured up to $250,000. The $250,000 insurance covers all accounts in your name at the same bank, not each CD or account you have at the bank.

As with all investments, there are benefits and risks associated with CDs. The disclosure statement should outline the interest rate on the CD and say if the rate is fixed or variable. It also should state when the bank pays interest on the CD, for example, monthly or semi-annually, and whether the interest payment will be made by check or by an electronic transfer of funds. The maturity date should be clearly stated, as should any penalties for the "early withdrawal" of the money in the CD. The risk with CDs is the risk that inflation will grow faster than your money, and lower your real returns over time.

Broker certificates of deposit

Although most CDs are purchased directly from banks, many brokerage firms and independent salespeople also offer CDs. These individuals and entities, known as "deposit brokers," can sometimes negotiate a higher rate of interest for a CD by promising to bring a certain amount of deposits to the institution. The deposit broker can then offer these "brokered CDs" to their customers.

Thoroughly check out the background of the issuer or deposit broker to ensure that the CD is from a reputable institution. Deposit brokers are not licensed or certified, and no state or federal agency approves them. Since anyone can claim to be a deposit broker, always check whether the deposit broker or the company he or she works for has a history of complaints or fraud. Many deposit brokers are affiliated with investment professionals. You can check out their disciplinary history using the SEC's and FINRA's online databases. Your state securities regulator may have additional information. To research the background of deposit brokers who are not affiliated with an investment firm, start by contacting your state's consumer protection office.

http://investor.gov/investing-basics/investment-products/certificates-deposit-cds [viii]

Section 5 - Commodities

What are commodities?

Commodity futures contracts are an agreement to buy or sell a specific quantity of a commodity at a specified price on a particular date in the future. Metals, grains, and other food, as well as financial instruments, including U.S. and foreign currencies, are traded in the futures market. With limited exceptions, trading in futures contracts must be executed on the floor of a commodity exchange. Exchange-traded commodity futures and options provide traders with contracts of a set unit size, a fixed expiration date, and centralized clearing. In centralized clearing, a clearing corporation acts as a single counterparty to every transaction and guarantees the completion and credit worthiness of all transactions.

Anyone who trades futures with the public or gives advice about futures trading must be registered with the National Futures Association (NFA). Before investing in commodity futures, check that the individual and firm are registered.

The SEC does not regulate commodity futures. The Commodity Futures Trading Commission (CFTC) is the federal agency that regulates futures trading. The CFTC cautions investors to be wary of offers for high yield investment opportunities in futures, options, or foreign exchange, also called forex. These are common areas of fraud.

For more information, please visit U.S. Commodity Futures Trading Commission.

Before you engage an investment professional or purchase commodities, make sure you research and verify all information: http://smartcheck.cftc.gov/.

http://investor.gov/investing-basics/investment-products/commodities [ix]

Section 6 - Corporate Bonds

A bond is a debt obligation, like an IOU. Investors who buy corporate bonds are lending money to the company issuing the bond. In return, the company makes a legal commitment to pay interest on the principal and, in most cases, to return the principal when the bond comes due, or matures.

To understand bonds, it is helpful to compare them with stocks. When you buy a share of common stock, you own equity in the company and will receive any dividends declared and paid by the company. When you buy a corporate bond, you do not own equity in the company. You will receive only the interest and principal on the bond, no matter how profitable the company becomes or how high its stock price climbs. But if the company runs into financial difficulties, it still has a legal obligation to make timely payments of interest and principal. The company has no similar obligation to pay dividends to shareholders. In a bankruptcy, bond investors have priority over shareholders in claims on the company's assets.

Like all investments, bonds carry risks. One key risk to a bondholder is that the company may fail to make timely payments of interest or principal. If that happens, the company will default on its bonds. This "default risk" makes the creditworthiness of the company—that is, its ability to pay its debt obligations on time—an important concern to bondholders.

What are the basic types of corporate bonds?

Corporate bonds make up one of the largest components of the U.S. bond market, which is considered the largest securities market in the world. Other components include U.S. Treasury bonds, other U.S. government bonds, and municipal bonds.

Companies use the proceeds from bond sales for a wide variety of purposes, including buying new equipment, investing in research and development, buying back their own stock, paying shareholder dividends, refinancing debt, and financing mergers and acquisitions.

Bonds can be classified according to their maturity, which is the date when the company has to pay back the principal to investors. Maturities can be short term (less than three years), medium term (four to 10 years), or long term (more than 10 years). Longer-term bonds usually offer higher interest rates, but may entail additional risks.

Bonds and the companies that issue them are also classified according to their credit quality. Credit rating agencies assign credit ratings based on their evaluation of the risk that the company may default on its bonds. Credit rating agencies periodically review their bond ratings and may revise them if conditions or expectations change.

Based on their credit ratings, bonds can be either *investment grade* or *non-investment grade*. Investment-grade bonds are considered more likely than non-investment grade bonds to be paid on time. Non-investment grade bonds, which are also called high-yield or speculative bonds, generally offer higher interest rates to compensate investors for greater risk.

Bonds also differ according to the type of interest payments they offer. Many bonds pay a *fixed rate* of interest throughout their term. Interest payments are called *coupon payments*, and the interest rate is called the coupon rate. With a fixed coupon rate, the coupon payments stay the same regardless of changes in market interest rates.

Other bonds offer *floating rates* that are reset periodically, such as every six months. These bonds adjust their interest payments to changes in market interest rates. Floating rates are based on a bond index or other benchmark. For example, the floating rate may equal the interest rate on a certain type of Treasury bond plus 1%.

One type of bond makes no interest payments until the bond matures. These are called *zero-coupon bonds*, because they make no coupon payments. Instead, the bond makes a single payment at maturity that is higher than the initial purchase price. For example, an investor may pay $800 to purchase a five-year, zero-coupon bond with a face value of $1,000. The company pays no interest on the bond for the next five years, and then, at maturity, pays $1,000—equal to the purchase price of $800 plus interest, or *original issue discount*, of $200. Investors in zero-coupon bonds generally must pay taxes each year on a prorated share of the interest before the interest is actually paid at maturity.

What happens if a company goes into bankruptcy?

If a company defaults on its bonds and goes bankrupt, bondholders will have a claim on the company's assets and cash flows. The bond's terms determine the bondholder's place in line, or the priority of the claim. Priority will be based on whether the bond is, for example, a secured bond, a senior unsecured bond or a junior unsecured (or subordinated) bond.

In the case of a *secured bond*, the company pledges specific collateral—such as property, equipment, or other assets that the company owns—as security for the bond. If the company defaults, holders of secured bonds will have a legal right to foreclose on the collateral to satisfy their claims.

Bonds that have no collateral pledged to them are *unsecured* and may be called *debentures*. Debentures have a general claim on the company's assets and cash flows. They may be classified as either *senior* or *junior (subordinated)* debentures. If the company defaults, holders of senior debentures will have a higher priority claim on the company's assets and cash flows than holders of junior debentures.

Bondholders, however, are usually not the company's only creditors. The company may also owe money to banks, suppliers, customers, pensioners, and others, some of whom may have equal or higher claims than certain bondholders. Sorting through the competing claims of creditors is a complex process that unfolds in bankruptcy court.

Additional information

Investor Bulletin: What are Corporate Bonds
Investor Bulletin: What are High-yield Corporate Bonds
Investor Bulletin: Interest Rate Risk
MSRB Investor Guide 2012
Bond Funds and Income Funds
Callable or Redeemable Bonds
Financial Industry Regulatory Authority

(FINRA)
Information on CUSIP numbers
Late Payment of Interest on Bonds
Municipal Securities Rulemaking Board (MSRB)
MSRB Electronic Municipal Market Access
(EMMA)
The Securities Industry and Financial Markets
Association (SIFMA)

[x]http://investor.gov/investing-basics/investment-products/corporate-bonds

Section 7 - Exchange-Traded Funds (ETFs)

This summary discusses only ETFs that are registered as open-end investment companies or unit investment trusts under the Investment Company Act of 1940 (the "1940 Act"). It does not address other types of exchange-traded products that are not registered under the 1940 Act, such as exchange-traded commodity funds or exchange-traded notes.

The following information is general in nature and is not intended to address the specifics of your financial situation. When considering an investment, make sure you understand the particular investment product fully before making an investment decision.

Summary of Topics Covered:

    a. What is an ETF?
    b. Things to Consider before Investing in ETFs
    c. Types of ETFs
    d. Final Words
    e. Additional Information

a. What is an ETF?

ETFs are a type of exchange-traded investment product that must register with the SEC under the 1940 Act as either an open-end investment company (generally known as "funds") or a unit investment trust.

Like mutual funds, ETFs offer investors a way to pool their money in a fund that makes investments in stocks, bonds, or other assets and, in return, to receive an interest in that investment pool. Unlike mutual funds, however, ETF shares are traded on a national stock exchange and at market prices that may or may not be the same as the net asset value ("NAV") of the shares, that is, the value of the ETF's assets minus its liabilities divided by the number of shares outstanding.

b. Things to Consider before Investing in ETFs

ETFs are not mutual funds. Generally, ETFs combine features of a mutual fund, which can be purchased or redeemed at the end of each trading day at its NAV per share, with the intraday trading feature of a closed-end fund, whose shares trade throughout the trading day at market prices.

Unlike with mutual fund shares, retail investors can only purchase and sell ETF shares in market transactions. That is, unlike mutual funds, ETFs do not sell individual shares directly to, or redeem their individual shares directly from, retail investors. Instead, ETF sponsors enter into contractual relationships with one or more financial institutions known as "Authorized Participants." Authorized Participants typically are large broker-dealers. Only Authorized Participants are permitted to purchase and redeem shares directly from the ETF, and they can do so only in large aggregations or blocks (*e.g.*, 50,000 ETF shares) commonly called "Creation Units."

Other investors purchase and sell ETF shares in market transactions at market prices. An ETF's market price typically will be more or less than the fund's NAV per share. This is because the ETF's market price fluctuates during the trading day as a result of a variety of factors, including the underlying prices of the ETF's assets and the demand for the ETF, while the ETF's NAV is the value of the ETF's assets minus its liabilities, as calculated by the ETF at the end of each business day.

c. Types of ETFs

Index-Based ETFs

Most ETFs trading in the marketplace are index-based ETFs. These ETFs seek to track a securities index like the S&P 500 stock index and generally invest primarily in the component securities of the index. For example, the SPDR, or "spider" ETF, which seeks to track the S&P 500 stock index, invests in most or all of the equity securities contained in the S&P 500 stock index. Some, but not all,

ETFs may post their holdings on their websites on a daily basis.

Actively Managed ETFs

Actively managed ETFs are not based on an index. Instead, they seek to achieve a stated investment objective by investing in a portfolio of stocks, bonds, and other assets. Unlike with an index-based ETF, an adviser of an actively managed ETF may actively buy or sell components in the portfolio on a daily basis without regard to conformity with an index.

d. Final words

Before investing in an ETF, you should read both its summary prospectus and its full prospectus, which provide detailed information on the ETF's investment objective, principal investment strategies, risks, costs, and historical performance (if any). The SEC's EDGAR system, as well as Internet search engines, can help you locate a specific ETF prospectus. You can also find prospectuses on the websites of the financial firms that sponsor a particular ETF, as well as through your broker.

Do not invest in something that you do not understand. If you cannot explain the investment opportunity in a few words and in an understandable way, you may need to reconsider the potential investment.

Finally, you may wish to consider seeking the advice of an investment professional. If you do, be sure to work with someone who understands your investment objectives and tolerance for risk. Your investment professional should understand complex products and be able to explain to your satisfaction whether or how they fit with your objectives.

e. Additional Information:

Investor Bulletin: Exchange-Traded Funds (ETFs)
SEC-FINRA Investor Alert on Leveraged and Inverse ETFs

SEC Fast Answers, Exchange-Traded Funds
FINRA Regulatory Notice 09-31
FINRA Non-Traditional ETFs FAQ

NYSE Informed Investor, What You Should Know About Exchange Traded Funds

http://investor.gov/investing-basics/investment-products/exchange-traded-funds-etfs [xi]

Section 8 - Hedge Funds

What are hedge funds?

Hedge funds pool money from investors and invest in securities or other types of investments with the goal of getting positive returns. Hedge funds are not regulated as heavily as mutual funds and generally have more leeway than mutual funds to pursue investments and strategies that may increase the risk of investment losses. Hedge funds are limited to wealthier investors who can afford the higher fees and risks of hedge fund investing, and institutional investors, including pension funds.

What should I know if I am considering investing in a hedge fund?

- **Be an accredited investor.** You generally must be an accredited investor, which means having a minimum level of income or assets, to invest in hedge funds.

- **Read a fund's prospectus and related materials.** Make sure you understand the level of risk involved in the fund's investment strategies, and that the risks are suitable to your personal investing goals, time horizons, and risk tolerance. As with any investment, the higher the potential returns, the higher the risks you must assume.

- **Understand how fund assets are valued.** Hedge funds may hold investments that are difficult to sell and may be difficult to value. You should understand the valuation process and know the extent to which a fund's holdings are valued by independent sources.

- **Understand fees.** Fees impact your return on investment. Hedge funds typically charge an asset management fee of 1-2% of assets, plus a "performance fee" of 20% of the hedge fund's profit. A performance fee could motivate a hedge fund manager to take greater risks in the hope of generating a larger return.

- **Understand any limitations on your right to redeem your shares.** Hedge funds typically limit opportunities to redeem, or cash in, your shares, to four times a year or less, and often impose a "lock-up" period of one year or more, during which you cannot cash in your shares.

- **Research hedge fund managers.** Make sure hedge fund managers are qualified to manage your money, and find out whether they have a disciplinary history within the securities industry.

- You can get this information by reviewing the adviser's Form ADV, which is the investment adviser's registration form. You can search for and view a firm's Form ADV using the SEC's Investment Adviser Public Disclosure (IAPD) website.

- If you don't find the investment adviser firm in the SEC's IAPD database, call your state securities regulator or search FINRA's BrokerCheck database.

- **Ask questions.** You are entrusting your money to someone else. You should know where your money is going, who is managing it, how it is being invested, and how you can get it back. In addition, you may wish to read FINRA's investor alert, which describes some of the risks of investing in funds of hedge funds.

Additional Information

Investor Bulletin: Hedge Funds
Using IAPD
Investor Bulletin: Amendments to Form ADV –
New Disclosure Requirements for Investment
Advisers

http://investor.gov/investing-basics/investment-products/hedge-funds [xii]

Section 9 - High-yield Corporate Bonds

A high-yield corporate bond is a type of corporate bond that offers a higher rate of interest because of its higher risk of default. When companies with a greater estimated default risk issue bonds, they may be unable to obtain an investment-grade bond credit rating. As a result, they typically issue bonds with higher interest rates in order to entice investors and compensate them for this higher risk.

High-yield bond issuers may be companies characterized as highly leveraged or those experiencing financial difficulties. Smaller or emerging companies may also have to issue high-yield bonds to offset unproven operating histories or because their financial plans may be considered speculative or risky.

For additional information, please visit the following links.

Investor Bulletin: What are Corporate Bonds
Investor Bulletin: What are High-yield Corporate Bonds
Investor Bulletin: Interest Rate Risk
MSRB Investor Guide 2012
Bond Funds and Income Funds
Callable or Redeemable Bonds
Financial Industry Regulatory Authority (FINRA)
Information on CUSIP numbers

Late Payment of Interest on Bonds
Municipal Securities Rulemaking Board (MSRB)
MSRB Electronic Municipal Market Access
(EMMA)
The Securities Industry and Financial Markets
Association (SIFMA)

http://investor.gov/investing-
basics/investment-products/high-yield-
corporate-bonds [xiii]

Section 10 - International Investing

Two of the chief reasons why people invest internationally are:

- **Diversification.** International investing may help U.S. investors to spread their investment risk to companies and markets that are outside of - and different than - the U.S. economy

- **Growth.** International investing takes advantage of the potential for faster growth in markets outside the U.S., particularly in emerging markets.

But there are special risks of international investing, including:

- **Changes in currency exchange rates.** When the exchange rate between the U.S. dollar and the currency of an international investment changes, it can increase or reduce your investment return.

- **Dramatic changes in market value.** All markets, including those outside the U.S., can experience dramatic changes in value.

- **Political, economic, and social events.** It is difficult for investors to understand all the political, economic, and social factors that influence markets, especially those abroad.

- **Lack of liquidity.** Markets outside the U.S. may have lower trading volumes and fewer listed companies. They may only be open a few hours a day. Some countries restrict the amount or type of stocks that foreign investors may purchase.

- **Less information.** Many companies outside the U.S. do not provide investors with the same type of information as U.S. public companies, and the information may not be available in English.

- **Foreign laws.** If you have a problem with your investment, you may not be able to sue the company in the U.S. Even if you sue successfully in a U.S. court, you may not be able to collect on a U.S. judgment against a non-U.S. company.

How can I invest internationally?

- **American Depositary Receipts.** The stocks of most non-U.S. companies that trade in the U.S. markets are traded as American Depositary Receipts (ADRs) issued by U.S. depositary banks. Each ADR represents one share of stock in a company outside the U.S. If you own an ADR you have the right to obtain the stock it represents, but U.S. investors usually find it more convenient to own the ADR. The price of an ADR corresponds to the price of the stock in its home market, adjusted for the ratio of ADRs to the company's shares.

- **Mutual Funds.** One way to invest internationally is through mutual funds. Mutual funds provide more diversification than most investors could achieve on their own. The fund will handle currency conversions and pay any foreign taxes, and is likely to understand the different operations of non-U.S. markets. There are different kinds of funds that invest internationally.

- **Global funds** invest primarily in companies outside the U.S., but may also invest in U.S. companies with international operations.

- **International funds** generally limit their investments to companies outside the U.S.

- **Regional or country funds** invest principally in companies located in a particular geographical region, such as

Asia or Europe, or in a single country. Some funds invest only in emerging markets while others concentrate on developed markets.

- **International index funds** try to track the results of a particular international market index. Index funds differ from actively managed funds, whose managers pick stocks based on research about the companies.

- **Trading on Foreign Markets.** If you want to buy or sell stock in a company that only trades outside the U.S., your broker may be able to process your order for you. These companies do not file reports with the SEC, so you will need to rely on other sources of information to make an investment decision. Always make sure any broker you deal with is registered with the SEC. It is against the law for brokers outside the U.S. who are not registered with the SEC to call you and solicit your investment.

Additional information

International Investing
SEC Office of International Affairs
Investor Bulletin: International Investing
Investor Bulletin: Foreign Currency Exchange
(Forex) Trading For Individual Investors

http://investor.gov/investing-
basics/investment-products/international-
investing [xiv]

Section 11 - Money Market Funds

What are money market funds?

Money market funds are a type of mutual fund developed in the 1970s as an option for investors to purchase a pool of securities that generally provided higher returns than interest-bearing bank accounts. They have since grown significantly and currently hold more than $2.9 trillion in assets, the majority of which is in institutional funds. There are many kinds of money market funds, including ones that invest primarily in government securities, tax-exempt municipal securities, or corporate debt securities. Money market funds that primarily invest in corporate debt securities are referred to as prime funds.

In response to the 2007-2008 financial crisis, the Commission adopted a series of amendments to its rules on money market funds in 2010 that were designed to make money market funds more resilient by reducing the interest rate, credit, and liquidity risks of their portfolios. Although these reforms improved money market fund resiliency, the Commission said at the time that it would continue to consider whether further, more fundamental changes to money market fund regulation might be warranted. Accordingly, on June 5, 2013, the Commission voted unanimously to propose additional measures that would reform the way that money market funds operate to make them less susceptible to runs that could harm investors.

The SEC's proposal includes two principal alternative reforms that could be adopted alone or in combination. One alternative would require a floating net asset value (NAV) for prime institutional money market funds. The other alternative would allow the use of liquidity fees and redemption gates in times of stress. The proposal also includes additional diversification and disclosure measures that would apply under either alternative.

On the money market funds spotlight page, you can find links to materials relating to SEC regulatory initiatives concerning money market funds, including the recently proposed rule, along with analysis, research, and other resources from the SEC. In addition, the money market funds spotlight page provides links to public comments received on the various rules and reports relating to money market funds.

Additional Information

Money Market Funds - SEC Spotlight
Topical Reference Guide - Money Market Funds
Money Market Fund Identification Information

http://investor.gov/investing-basics/investment-products/money-market-funds

Section 12 - Municipal Bonds

What are municipal bonds?

Municipal bonds (or "Munis" for short) are debt securities issued by states, cities, counties and other governmental entities to fund day-to-day obligations and to finance capital projects such as building schools, highways or sewer systems. By purchasing municipal bonds, you are in effect lending money to the bond issuer in exchange for a promise of regular interest payments, usually semi-annually, and the return of the original investment, or "principal." A municipal bond's maturity date (the date when the issuer of the bond repays the principal) may be years in the future. Short-term bonds mature in one to three years, while long-term bonds won't mature for more than a decade.

Generally, the interest on municipal bonds is exempt from federal income tax. The interest may also be exempt from state and local taxes if you reside in the state where the bond is issued. Bond investors typically seek a steady stream of income payments and, compared to stock investors, may be more risk-averse and more focused on preserving, rather than increasing, wealth. Given the tax benefits, the interest rate for municipal bonds is usually lower than on taxable fixed-income securities such as corporate bonds.

The two most common types of municipal bonds are the following:

- **General obligation bonds** are issued by states, cities or counties and not secured by any assets. Instead, general obligation are backed by the "full faith and credit" of the issuer, which has the power to tax residents to pay bondholders.

- **Revenue bonds** are not backed by government's taxing power but by revenues from a specific project or source, such as highway tolls or lease fees. Some revenue bonds are "non-recourse", meaning that if the revenue stream dries up, the bondholders do not have a claim on the underlying revenue source.

In addition, municipal borrowers sometimes issue bonds on behalf of private entities such as non-profit colleges or hospitals. These "conduit" borrowers typically agree to repay the issuer, who pays the interest and principal on the bonds. In cases where the conduit borrower fails to make a payment, the issuer usually is not required to pay the bondholders.

Where can investors find information about municipal bonds?

Investors wishing to research municipal bonds may access a range of information online free of charge at the Municipal Securities Rulemaking Board's Electronic Municipal Market Access (EMMA) website. Information available to you includes:

- Disclosure documents going back as early as 1990, including a bond's official statement, which is a disclosure document similar to a prospectus that includes important characteristics, such as type, yield, maturity, credit quality, call features and risk factors, as well as audited financial statements, material event notices and other continuing disclosures (including ratings changes, principal and interest payment delinquencies and non-payment related defaults).[1]

- Historical and real-time transaction price data, including information relating to a type of municipal bond called a "variable rate demand obligation" that resets its interest rate periodically. Investors should be aware that recent price information may not be available for bonds that do not trade frequently.[2]

What are some of the risks of investing in municipal bonds?

As with any investment, investing in municipal bonds entails risk. Investors in municipal bonds face a number of risks, specifically including:

Call risk. Call risk refers to the potential for an issuer to repay a bond before its maturity date, something that an issuer may do if interest rates decline -- much as a homeowner might refinance a mortgage loan to benefit from lower interest rates. Bond calls are less likely when interest rates are stable or moving higher. Many municipal bonds are "callable," so investors who want to hold a municipal bond to maturity should research the bond's call provisions before making a purchase.

Credit risk. This is the risk that the bond issuer may experience financial problems that make it difficult or impossible to pay interest and principal in full (the failure to pay interest or principal is referred to as "default"). Credit ratings are available for many bonds. Credit ratings seek to estimate the relative credit risk of a bond as compared with other bonds, although a high rating does not reflect a prediction that the bond has no chance of defaulting.

Interest rate risk. Bonds have a fixed face value, known as the "par" value. If bonds are held to maturity, the investor will receive the face value amount back, plus interest that may be set at a fixed or floating rate. The bond's market price will move up as interest rates move down and it will decline as interest rates rise, so that the market value of the bond may be more or less than the par value. U.S. interest rates have been low for some time. If they move higher, investors who hold a low fixed-rate municipal bond and try to sell it before it matures could lose money because of the lower market value of the bond.

Inflation risk. Inflation is a general upward movement in prices. Inflation reduces purchasing power, which is a risk for investors receiving a fixed rate of interest. It also can lead to higher interest rates and, in turn, lower market value for existing bonds.

Liquidity risk. This refers to the risk that investors won't find an active market for the municipal bond, potentially preventing them from buying or selling when they want and obtaining a certain price for the bond. Many investors buy municipal bonds to hold them rather than to trade them, so the market for a particular bond may not be especially liquid and quoted prices for the same bond may differ.

In addition to the risks, what other factors should you consider when investing in municipal bonds?

Tax implications. Consider consulting a tax professional to discuss the bond's tax implications, including the possibility that your bond may be subject to the federal alternative minimum tax or eligible for state income tax benefits.

Broker compensation. Most brokers are compensated through a markup over the cost of the bond to the firm. This markup is usually not disclosed on your confirmation statement. If a commission is charged, it will be reported on your confirmation statement. You should ask your broker about markups and commissions.

The background of the broker or adviser selling the bond. A securities salesperson must be properly licensed, and, depending on the type of business the firm conducts, his or her firm must be registered with the MSRB and with FINRA, the SEC or a state securities regulator. You can check out an investment adviser on the SEC's Investment Adviser Public Disclosure website at www.adviserinfo.sec.gov and a broker on FINRA's BrokerCheck website at www.finra.org/brokercheck. To confirm MSRB registration, you can review the MSRB's

registered dealers list
at http://www.msrb.org/msrb1/pqweb/registra
nts.asp.

[1] Official statements produced before June
1, 2009 and continuing disclosure documents
produced before July 1, 2009, may be available
from one of the following
organizations: Bloomberg Municipal
Repository, DPC Data, Interactive Data Pricing
and Reference Data or Standard & Poor's.
These organizations may charge a fee.

[2] FINRA's Market Data Center also offers
price and trade information
at www.finra.org/marketdata.

Related Information

Investor Bulletin: Municipal Bonds (March 2012)

Investor Bulletin: Focus on Municipal Bonds (September 2010)

Investor Bulletin: New Rules for Improving Municipal Disclosure

Using EMMA - Researching Municipal Securities and 529 Plans

FINRA and MSRB Investor Alert: Municipal Bonds—Staying on the Safe Side of the Street in Rough Times

SEC's Office of Municipal Securities

Spotlight on Municipal Securities Markets

Municipal Securities Rulemaking Board EMMA Education Center

Municipal Securities Rulemaking Board Electronic Municipal Market Access (EMMA)

http://investor.gov/investing-basics/investment-products/municipal-bonds xv

Section 13 - Mutual Funds

What are mutual funds?

A mutual fund is a company that pools money from many investors and invests the money in securities such as stocks, bonds, and short-term debt. The combined holdings of the mutual fund are known as its portfolio. Investors buy shares in mutual funds. Each share represents an investor's part ownership in the fund and the income it generates.

Summary of Topics Covered:

a. Why do people buy mutual funds?
b. What types of mutual funds are there?
c. What are the benefits and risks of mutual funds?
d. How to buy and sell mutual funds
e. Understanding fees
f. Avoiding fraud
g. Additional information

a. Why do people buy mutual funds?

Mutual funds are a popular choice among investors because they generally offer the following features:

- **Professional Management.** The fund managers do the research for you. They select the securities and monitor the performance.

- **Diversification** or "Don't put all your eggs in one basket." Mutual funds typically invest in a range of companies and industries. This helps to lower your risk if one company fails.

- **Affordability.** Most mutual funds set a relatively low dollar amount for initial investment and subsequent purchases.

- **Liquidity.** Mutual fund investors can easily redeem their shares at any time, for the current net asset value (NAV) plus any redemption fees.

b. What types of mutual funds are there?

Most mutual funds fall into one of four main categories – money market funds, bond funds, stock funds, and target date funds. Each type has different features, risks, and rewards.

- **Money market funds** have relatively low risks. By law, they can invest only in certain high-quality, short-term investments issued by U.S. corporations, and federal, state and local governments.

- **Bond funds** have higher risks than money market funds because they typically aim to produce higher returns. Because there are many different types of bonds, the risks and rewards of bond funds can vary dramatically.

- **Stock funds** invest in corporate stocks. Not all stock funds are the same. Some examples are:

  - Growth funds focus on stocks that may not pay a regular dividend but have potential for above-average financial gains.

  - Income funds invest in stocks that pay regular dividends.

  - Index funds track a particular market index such as the Standard & Poor's 500 Index.

  - Sector funds specialize in a particular industry segment.

- **Target date funds** hold a mix of stocks, bonds, and other investments. Over time, the mix gradually shifts according to the fund's strategy. Target date funds, sometimes known as lifecycle funds, are designed for individuals with particular retirement dates in mind.

c. What are the benefits and risks of mutual funds?

Mutual funds offer professional investment management and potential diversification. They also offer three ways to earn money:

- **Dividend Payments.** A fund may earn income from dividends on stock or interest on bonds. The fund then pays the shareholders nearly all the income, less expenses.

- **Capital Gains Distributions.** The price of the securities in a fund may increase. When a fund sells a security that has increased in price, the fund has a capital gain. At the end of the year, the fund distributes these capital gains, minus any capital losses, to investors.

- **Increased NAV.** If the market value of a fund's portfolio increases, after deducting expenses, then the value of the fund and its shares increases. The higher NAV reflects the higher value of your investment.

All funds carry some level of risk. With mutual funds, you may lose some or all of the money you invest because the securities held by a fund can go down in value. Dividends or interest payments may also change as market conditions change.

A fund's past performance is not as important as you might think because past performance does not predict future returns. But past performance can tell you how volatile or stable a fund has been over a period of time. The more volatile the fund, the higher the investment risk.

d. How to buy and sell mutual funds

Investors buy mutual fund shares from the fund itself or through a broker for the fund, rather than from other investors. The price that investors pay for the mutual fund is the funds per share net asset value plus any fees charged at the time of purchase, such as sales loads.

Mutual fund shares are "redeemable," meaning investors can sell the shares back to the fund at any time. The fund usually must send you the payment within seven days.

Before buying shares in a mutual fund, read the prospectus carefully. The prospectus contains information about the mutual fund's investment objectives, risks, performance, and expenses.

e. Understanding fees

As with any business, running a mutual fund involves costs. Funds pass along these costs to investors by charging fees and expenses. Fees and expenses vary from fund to fund. A fund with high costs must perform better than a low-cost fund to generate the same returns for you.

Even small differences in fees can mean large differences in returns over time. For example, if you invested $10,000 in a fund with a 10% annual return, and annual operating expenses of 1.5%, after 20 years you would have roughly $49,725. If you invested in a fund with the same performance and expenses of 0.5%, after 20 years you would end up with $60,858.

It takes only minutes to use a mutual fund cost calculator to compute how the costs of different mutual funds add up over time and eat into your returns. See the Mutual Fund Glossary for types of fees.

f. Avoiding fraud

By law, each mutual fund is required to file a prospectus and regular shareholder reports with the SEC. Before you invest, be sure to read the prospectus and the required shareholder reports. Additionally, the investment portfolios of mutual funds are managed by separate entities known as "investment advisers" that are registered with the SEC. Always check that the investment adviser is registered before investing.

g. Additional Information

Mutual Funds - A Guide for Investors
Closed-End Funds
Index Funds
Interval Funds
Mutual Fund Proxy Voting Records and Policies
Mutual Fund Investing: Look at More Than a
Fund's Past Performance

http://investor.gov/investing-
basics/investment-products/mutual-funds [xvi]

Section 14 - Real Estate Investment Trusts (REITs)

What are REITs?

Real estate investment trusts ("REITs") allow individuals to invest in large-scale, income-producing real estate. A REIT is a company that owns and typically operates income-producing real estate or related assets. These may include office buildings, shopping malls, apartments, hotels, resorts, self-storage facilities, warehouses, and mortgages or loans. Unlike other real estate companies, a REIT does not develop real estate properties to resell them. Instead, a REIT buys and develops properties primarily to operate them as part of its own investment portfolio.

Why would somebody invest in REITs?

REITs provide a way for individual investors to earn a share of the income produced through commercial real estate ownership – without actually having to go out and buy commercial real estate.

What types of REITs are there?

Many REITs are registered with the SEC and are publicly traded on a stock exchange. These are known as publicly traded REITs. Others may be registered with the SEC but are not publicly traded. These are known as non-traded REITs (also known as non-exchange traded REITs). This is one of the most important distinctions among the various kinds of REITs. Before investing in a REIT, you should understand whether or not it is publicly traded, and how this could affect the benefits and risks to you.

What are the benefits and risks of REITs?

REITs offer a way to include real estate in one's investment portfolio. Additionally, some REITs may offer higher dividend yields than some other investments.

But there are some risks, especially with non-exchange traded REITs. Because they do not trade on a stock exchange, non-traded REITs involve special risks:

- **Lack of Liquidity:** Non-traded REITs are illiquid investments. They generally cannot be sold readily on the open market. If you need to sell an asset to raise money quickly, you may not be able to do so with shares of a non-traded REIT.

- **Share Value Transparency:** While the market price of a publicly traded REIT is readily accessible, it can be difficult to determine the value of a share of a non-traded REIT. Non-traded REITs typically do not provide an estimate of their value per share until 18 months after their offering closes. This may be years after you have made your investment. As a result, for a significant time period you may be unable to assess the value of your non-traded REIT investment and its volatility.

- **Distributions May Be Paid from Offering Proceeds and Borrowings:** Investors may be attracted to non-traded REITs by their relatively high dividend yields compared to those of publicly traded REITs. Unlike publicly traded REITs, however, non-traded REITs frequently pay distributions in excess of their funds from operations. To do so, they may use offering proceeds and borrowings. This practice, which is typically not used by publicly traded REITs, reduces the value of the shares and the cash available to the company to purchase additional assets.

- **Conflicts of Interest:** Non-traded REITs typically have an external manager instead of their own employees. This can lead to potential conflicts of interests with shareholders. For example, the REIT may pay the external manager significant fees based on the amount of property acquisitions and assets under management. These fee incentives may not necessarily align with the interests of shareholders.

How to buy and sell REITs

You can invest in a publicly traded REIT, which is listed on a major stock exchange, by purchasing shares through a broker. You can purchase shares of a non-traded REIT through a broker that participates in the non-traded REIT's offering. You can also purchase shares in a REIT mutual fund or REIT exchange-traded fund.

Understanding fees and taxes

Publicly traded REITs can be purchased through a broker. Generally, you can purchase the common stock, preferred stock, or debt security of a publicly traded REIT. Brokerage fees will apply.

Non-traded REITs are typically sold by a broker or financial adviser. Non-traded REITs generally have high up-front fees. Sales commissions and upfront offering fees usually total approximately 9 to 10 percent of the investment. These costs lower the value of the investment by a significant amount.

Special Tax Considerations

Most REITS pay out at least 100 percent of their taxable income to their shareholders. The shareholders of a REIT are responsible for paying taxes on the dividends and any capital gains they receive in connection with their investment in the REIT. Dividends paid by REITs generally are treated as ordinary income and are not entitled to the reduced tax rates on other types of corporate dividends. Consider consulting your tax adviser before investing in REITs.

Avoiding fraud

Be wary of any person who attempts to sell REITs that are not registered with the SEC.

You can verify the registration of both publicly traded and non-traded REITs through the SEC's EDGAR system. You can also use EDGAR to review a REIT's annual and quarterly reports as well as any offering prospectus. For more on how to use EDGAR, please visit Research Public Companies.

You should also check out the broker or investment adviser who recommends purchasing a REIT. To learn how to do so, please visit Working with Brokers and Investment Advisers.

Additional information

SEC Investor Bulletin: Real Estate Investment Trusts (REITs)

FINRA Investor Alert: Public Non-Traded REITs - Perform a Careful Review Before Investing

http://investor.gov/investing-basics/investment-products/real-estate-investment-trusts-reits [xvii]

Section 15 - Savings Bonds

Savings bonds are debt securities issued by the U.S. Department of the Treasury to help pay for the U.S. government's borrowing needs. U.S. savings bonds are considered one of the safest investments because they are backed by the full faith and credit of the U.S. government.

Starting January 1, 2012, you can no longer buy paper savings bonds at financial institutions. But you can go online to purchase two types of electronic savings bonds. Under the rules, an individual can buy a maximum of $10,000 worth in each series in a single calendar year, or a total of $20,000.

Series EE U.S. Savings Bonds are an appreciation-type (or accrual-type) savings security. They are sold at face value, so you'll pay $50 for a $50 bond. The bond is worth its full value upon redemption. The interest is issued electronically to your designated account. You cannot buy more than $10,000 (face value) of Series EE bonds in any calendar year. If you redeem the bonds in the first five years of buying them, you'll forfeit interest payments for the three most recent months. After five years, you won't be penalized for redemptions.

Series I U.S. Savings Bonds are inflation-indexed. They are sold at face value and you can buy up to $10,000 (face value) of Series I bonds in any calendar year. Series I Bonds offer a fixed rate of interest, adjusted for inflation. As with Series EE Bonds, if you redeem Series I Bonds in the first five years, you'll forfeit the three most recent months' interest. After five years, you won't be penalized for redemptions.

Key advantages of savings bonds include:

- **Popularity as gifts**. Savings bonds are a popular birthday and graduation gift and also can be used toward financing education, supplemental retirement income, and other special events. Unlike other securities, minors may hold U.S. savings bonds in their own name.

- **Tax advantages**. You pay no state or local taxes on the interest on the bonds, and you can defer paying federal taxes on the interest until you cash in the bond or until it matures. In addition, tax benefits are available for eligible taxpayers when Series EE and Series I savings bonds are used for qualified education expenses. For details on the education tax exclusion and the requirements to qualify visit, http://www.treasurydirect.gov/indiv/plan ning/plan_education.htm.

You can buy these electronic savings bonds in penny increments, from $25 up to $5,000 each year. (In paper form, these bonds were only available in specific denominations.) For more on the switch to all-electronic savings bonds and on how to open a TreasuryDirect account, please visit this page at TreasuryDirect.gov. You can use the Savings Bond Calculator and compare the different types of securities issued by the Treasury.

http://investor.gov/investing-basics/investment-products/savings-bonds [xviii]

Section 16 – Stocks

What are stocks?

Stocks are a type of security that gives stockholders a share of ownership in a company. Stocks also are called "equities."

Summary of Topics Covered:

a. Why do people buy stocks?
b. Why do companies issue stock?
c. What kinds of stock are there?
d. What are the benefits and risks of stocks?
e. How to buy and sell stocks
f. Understanding fees
g. Avoiding fraud
h. Additional information

a. Why do people buy stocks?

Investors buy stocks for various reasons. Here are some of them:

- Capital appreciation, which occurs when a stock rises in price

- Dividend payments, which come when the company distributes some of its earnings to stockholders

- Ability to vote shares and influence the company

b. Why do companies issue stock?

Companies issue stock to get money for various things, which may include:

- Paying off debt
- Launching new products
- Expanding into new markets or regions
- Enlarging facilities or building new ones

c. What kinds of stocks are there?

There are two main kinds of stocks, common stock and preferred stock.

Common stock entitles owners to vote at shareholder meetings and receive dividends.

Preferred stockholders usually don't have voting rights but they receive dividend payments before common stockholders do, and have priority over common stockholders if the company goes bankrupt and its assets are liquidated.

Common and preferred stocks may fall into one or more of the following categories:

- **Growth stocks** have earnings growing at a faster rate than the market average. They rarely pay dividends and investors buy them in the hope of capital appreciation. A start-up technology company is likely to be a growth stock.

- **Income stocks** pay dividends consistently. Investors buy them for the income they generate. An established utility company is likely to be an income stock.

- **Value stocks** have a low price-to-earnings (PE) ratio, meaning they are cheaper to buy than stocks with a higher PE. Value stocks may be growth or income stocks, and their low PE ratio may reflect the fact that they have fallen out of favor with investors for some reason. People buy value stocks in the hope that the market has overreacted and that the stock's price will rebound.

- **Blue-chip stocks** are shares in large, well-known companies with a solid history of growth. They generally pay dividends.

Another way to categorize stocks is by the size of the company, as shown in its market capitalization. There are large-cap, mid-cap, and small-cap stocks. Shares in very small companies are sometimes called "microcap" stocks. The very lowest priced stocks are known as "penny stocks." These companies may have little or no earnings. Penny stocks do not pay dividends and are highly speculative.

d. What are the benefits and risks of stocks?

Stocks offer investors the greatest potential for growth (capital appreciation) over the long haul. Investors willing to stick with stocks over long periods of time, say 15 years, generally have been rewarded with strong, positive returns.

But stock prices move down as well as up. There's no guarantee that the company whose stock you hold will grow and do well, so you can lose money you invest in stocks.

If a company goes bankrupt and its assets are liquidated, common stockholders are the last in line to share in the proceeds. The company's bondholders will be paid first, then holders of preferred stock. If you are a common stockholder, you get whatever is left, which may be nothing.

Even when companies aren't in danger of failing, their stock price may fluctuate up or down. Large company stocks as a group, for example, have lost money on average about one out of every three years. If you have to sell shares on a day when the stock price is below the price you paid for the shares, you will lose money on the sale.

Market fluctuations can be unnerving to some investors. A stock's price can be affected by factors inside the company, such as a faulty product, or by events the company has no control over, such as political or market events.

Stocks usually are one part of an investor's holdings. If you are young and saving for a long-term goal such as retirement, you may want to hold more stocks than bonds. Investors nearing or in retirement may want to hold more bonds than stocks.

The risks of stock holdings can be offset in part by investing in a number of different stocks. Investing in other kinds of assets that are not stocks, such as bonds, is another way to offset some of the risks of owning stocks.

e. How to buy and sell stocks

You can buy and sell stocks through:

- A direct stock plan
- A dividend reinvestment plan
- A discount or full-service broker
- A stock fund

Direct stock plans. Some companies allow you to buy or sell their stock directly through them without using a broker. This saves on commissions, but you may have to pay other fees to the plan, including if you transfer shares to a broker to sell them. Some companies limit direct stock plans to employees of the company or existing shareholders. Some require minimum amounts for purchases or account levels.

Direct stock plans usually will not allow you to buy or sell shares at a specific market price or at a specific time. Instead, the company will buy or sell shares for the plan at set times — such as daily, weekly, or monthly — and at an average market price. Depending on the plan, you may be able to automate your purchases and have the cost deducted automatically from your savings account.

Dividend reinvestment plans. These plans allow you to buy more shares of a stock you already own by reinvesting dividend payments into the company. You must sign an agreement with the company to have this done. Check with the company or your brokerage firm to see if you will be charged for this service.

Discount or full-service broker. Brokers buy and sell shares for customers for a fee, known as a commission.

Stock funds are another way to buy stocks. These are a type of mutual fund that invests primarily in stocks. Depending on its investment objective and policies, a stock fund may concentrate on a particular type of stock, such as blue chips, large-cap value stocks, or mid-cap growth stocks. Stock funds are offered by investment companies and can be purchased directly from them or through a broker or adviser.

f. Understanding fees

Buying and selling stocks entails fees. A direct stock plan or a dividend reinvestment plan may charge you a fee for that service. Brokers who buy and sell stocks for you charge a commission. A discount brokerage charges lower commissions than what you would pay at a full-service brokerage. But generally you have to research and choose investments by yourself. A full-service brokerage costs more, but the higher commissions pay for investment advice based on that firm's research.

g. Avoiding fraud

Stocks in public companies are registered with the SEC and in most cases, public companies are required to file reports to the SEC quarterly and annually. Annual reports include financial statements that have been audited by an independent audit firm. Information on public companies can be found on the SEC's EDGAR system.

h. Additional information

http://investor.gov/investing-basics/investment-products/stocks [xix]

Section 17 - Structured Notes with Principal Protection

The retail market for structured notes with principal protection has been growing in recent years. While these products often have reassuring names that include some variant of "principal protection," "capital guarantee," "absolute return," "minimum return" or similar terms, they are not risk-free. Any promise to repay some or all of the money you invest will depend on the creditworthiness of the issuer of the note—meaning you could lose all of your money if the issuer of your note goes bankrupt.

Summary of Topics Covered:

a. What Are Structured Notes with Principal Protection?
b. How Do These Notes Protect My Investment?
c. How Do Structured Notes with Principal Protection Calculate the Return on My Investment?
d. Can I Get My Money When I Need It?
e. Do Structured Notes with Principal Protection Have Fees?
f. What Other Costs or Tradeoffs Are Involved?
g. How Are These Products Taxed?
h. What Questions Should I Ask Before

Investing?
i. Additional Resources

http://investor.gov/investing-
basics/investment-products/structured-notes-
principal-protection [xx]

**Structured Notes with Principal
Protection: Note the Terms of Your
Investment**

The retail market for structured notes with
principal protection has been growing in recent
years. While these products often have
reassuring names that include some variant of
"principal protection," "capital guarantee,"
"absolute return," "minimum return" or similar
terms, they are not risk-free. Any promise to
repay some or all of the money you invest will
depend on the creditworthiness of the issuer of
the note—meaning you could lose all of your
money if the issuer of your note goes
bankrupt. Also, some of these products have
conditions to the protection or offer only partial
protection, so you could lose principal even if
the issuer does not go bankrupt. And you
typically will receive principal protection from
the issuer only if you hold your note until
maturity. If you need to cash out your note
before maturity, you should be aware that this
might not be possible if no secondary market
to sell your note exists and the issuer refuses
to redeem it. Even where a secondary market

exists, the note may be quite illiquid and you could receive substantially less than your purchase price.

While structured notes with principal protection have the potential to outperform the total interest payment that would be paid on typical fixed interest rate bonds, these notes also might underperform a typical fixed interest rate bond and could earn no return for the entire term of the note, even if you hold the note to maturity. Their terms and structures also can be more complex than traditional bonds, making them more difficult for investors to evaluate. Finally, as with structured products generally, structured notes with principal protection may have hidden or imputed costs that can be relatively high and difficult to understand.

FINRA and the SEC's Office of Investor Education and Advocacy are issuing this alert to make investors aware of these risks and to help them better understand how structured notes with principal protection work. The alert includes questions investors should ask when considering structured notes with principal protection and provides links to helpful resources, including a recent FINRA Regulatory Notice on these products. In particular, the terms related to any protections to or guarantee of your principal require a careful review.

a. What Are Structured Notes with Principal Protection?

For the purposes of this alert, the term "structured note with principal protection" refers to any structured product that combines a bond with a derivative component—and that offers a full or partial return of principal at maturity. Structured products in general do not represent ownership of any portfolio of assets but rather are promises to pay made by the product issuers. Structured notes with principal protection typically reflect the combination of a zero-coupon bond, which pays no interest until the bond matures, with an option or other derivative product whose payoff is linked to an underlying asset, index or benchmark. The underlying asset, index or benchmark can vary widely from commonly cited market benchmarks to foreign equity indices, currencies, commodities, spreads between interest rates or "hybrid" baskets of various asset types. For example, a note might be based on the performance of an equally weighted basket composed of the Russell 2000, an exchange-traded fund tracking a real estate index, the Brazilian Real-U.S. Dollar exchange rate and the price of copper. These products are designed to return some or all principal at a set maturity date—typically ranging up to 10 years from issuance. The investor also is entitled to participate in a return that is linked to a specified change in the value of the underlying asset.

b. How Do These Notes Protect My Investment?

If you hold a structured note with principal protection until maturity, you typically will get back at least some—and perhaps all—of your initial investment, even if the underlying asset, index or benchmark declines. Be aware that protection levels may vary. While some products return 100 percent of principal at maturity, others return as little as 10 percent. In some cases, the principal protection does not apply unless some contingency is met—sometimes called "contingent protection"—so it may provide no protection at all, even if the sales materials suggest otherwise.

Also, any guarantee that your principal will be protected—whether in whole or in part—is only as good as the financial strength of the company that makes that promise. In other words, the principal guarantee is subject to the creditworthiness of the guarantor, which is generally the securities firm that structures and issues the note. In the event the issuer goes bankrupt, investors who hold these notes are considered unsecured creditors and might recover little, if anything, of their original investment. This is what happened to investors who purchased structured notes with principal protection issued by now bankrupt Lehman Brothers Holdings.

c. How Do Structured Notes with Principal Protection Calculate the Return on My Investment?

Some structured notes with principal protection make periodic interest payments while others don't. The return on your investment—over and above any principal guarantee and assuming you hold the note to maturity—will depend on a host of factors, including the method the issuer uses to calculate gains (or losses) linked to the performance of the underlying asset, index or benchmark (the "market-linked" returns), the note's participation rate and any minimum guaranteed return.

Market-linked gains (or losses). As with other complex financial products, there can be varying and often complicated methods of calculating a market-linked gain or loss. For example, one product might compare the change in an index at two discrete points in time, such as the beginning and ending dates of the note's term (point-to-point). Another product might look at the index value at various points during the life of the investment, for example at annual anniversaries, and then compare the highest value with the value of the index level at the start of the term (high water mark). Some products base your return on the number of days during the holding period that the underlying index stayed above (or below) a pre-specified level (accrual)—or within a range of pre-specified levels (range). And still others use complex, conditional formulas that allow you to participate in some or all of the index's gain up to a set level—but significantly limit your return if, at any time during the holding period, the index rises above that level (shark fin).

Participation rates. A participation rate determines how much of the gain in the underlying asset, index or benchmark will be credited to the note. For example, if the participation rate is 75 percent, and the asset, index or benchmark increases 10 percent, then the return credited to your note would be 7.5 percent.

Minimum guaranteed returns. If a structured note with principal protection offers a "minimum guaranteed return," be sure to carefully read the prospectus to understand how the issuer defines that term. In some instances, the term includes not only the principal guarantee but also a fixed overall investment return. For example, a note with 100 percent return of principal at maturity and a 2 percent minimum guaranteed return would pay out 102 percent of your initial investment at maturity, regardless of how the underlying asset, index or benchmark performed. In other cases, however, an issuer might use the term to refer only to the level of principal protection.

The bottom line for investors is that structured notes with principal protection can have complicated pay-out structures that can make it hard to accurately assess their risk and potential for growth. In addition, depending on how the note is structured, the distinct possibility exists that you could tie up your principal for upwards of a decade with the possibility of no profit on your initial investment. While your principal might be returned at maturity, that might be all you get back after this lengthy holding period—and, in the meantime, inflation could erode your purchasing power.

The chart below illustrates a hypothetical example of one of the more complex pay-out structures, sometimes referred to as a "shark fin" pay-out.

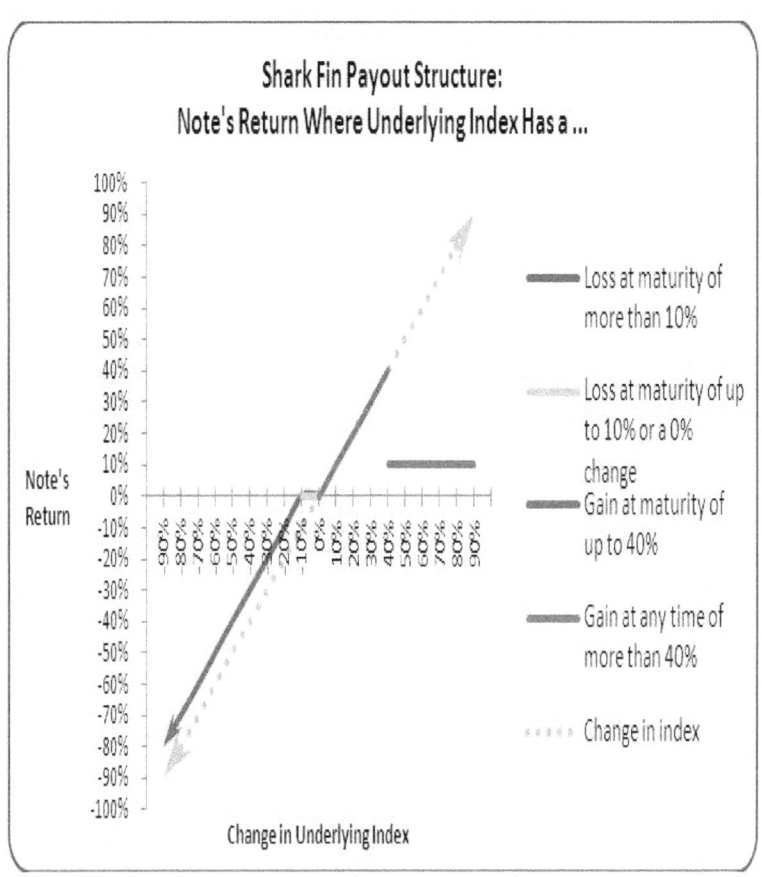

Shark Fin Pay-out Assumptions:

Principal protection of 10 percent of
initial investment
100 percent participation in index gains
up to 40 percent, so the maximum
return is 140 percent of principal
Automatic 110 percent return at maturity
if the index gains more than 40 percent
at any time during the life of the note

As the shark fin hypothetical above demonstrates, a note might be structured in a way that your upside exposure to the underlying asset, index or benchmark is limited or capped, which is generally a tradeoff for offering the principal protection. Although it might seem counterintuitive, in the example above, a 40 percent gain in the underlying index results in the return of 140 percent of principal invested, while a 41 percent gain (achieved at any time) would automatically result in the return of only 110 percent at maturity. This shows why reading and understanding the terms of these notes is so important.

d. Can I Get My Money When I Need It?

Potential lack of liquidity is one of the disadvantages of structured notes with principal protection. These products tend to be longer-term investments, tying up your money for several years. Some issuers might allow investors to redeem their notes before maturity under certain circumstances, such as expiration of a "lock-up period" (a period of time during which you cannot access your funds), payment of a redemption fee or both. Other issuers might (but are not obligated to) provide a secondary market for certain notes. However, depending on demand, the notes might trade at significant discounts to their purchase price and might not return the full guaranteed amount. In addition, the value of the note before maturity might be difficult to calculate and can vary depending a wide array of factors (including prevailing interest rates and the volatility of the underlying asset, index or benchmark). You might also have to pay a penalty for early redemption, further reducing any return of your principal.

> **Be aware of call risk.** Call risk refers to the possibility that the issuer could call or redeem your note before maturity. This generally happens when it is in the issuer's—rather than the investor's—best interest to do so, such as when interest rates fall. While the bond's principal is repaid early, you might be unable to find a similar investment with as attractive a yield.

e. Do Structured Notes with Principal Protection Have Fees?

Yes, even if the sales materials suggest otherwise. Virtually every investment has either implicit or explicit fees, whether they are described as selling commissions or concessions, management fees, structuring fees, early redemption fees or by some other term.

f. What Other Costs or Tradeoffs Are Involved?

Depending on their terms and the way they are put together, structured notes with principal protection can have hidden or imputed costs, which in some cases may be relatively high. These stem from the way a product is "bundled" or "packaged." At issuance, any given note will have an estimated fair value based on its structure. The issuer generally raises this value by a spread to arrive at the offering price of the product, which captures costs to the issuer associated with the note over its life, such as costs of hedging, as well as the issuer's profit. The hidden costs of purchasing virtually any structured product include the possibility that you could have assembled a similar bundle of investments on your own at a lower cost—and potentially with higher returns. The maximum return of any particular structured note with principal protection will typically reflect (and account for) the issuer's costs of manufacturing and maintaining the note as well as its own profit margin. These costs generally are not transparent to investors.

Other costs of investing in structured notes with principal protection include the opportunity cost involved with sacrificing a potentially higher yield to obtain some downside protection. It is also important to note that the principal protection generally relates to nominal principal and does not offer inflation protection. And, for any underlying investment that would ordinarily pay dividends, structured notes, like other equity or index-linked investments, typically exclude dividends.

g. How Are These Products Taxed?

In most cases, if you invest in a structured note with principal protection, you must pay federal taxes while you own the product, even before maturity or during any lock-up period and even if you haven't received any cash payments. This can occur if the interest on the product's zero-coupon bond holdings (resulting from the principal guarantee) is considered to be imputed interest for federal income tax purposes. You should read the tax consequences description in the prospectus and consult your tax advisor to know how a particular structured note might be taxed and when you must report any income or loss.

h. What Questions Should I Ask Before Investing?

When you evaluate a structured note with principal protection, be sure to do your research to find answers to the following questions, among others, or ask your investment professional:

How do I know whether this product is appropriate for me given my overall investment objectives? What is the level of principal protection offered? There is a big difference between 100 percent return of principal and 10 percent return, or something in between. Know your protection percentage.

Are there conditions to the principal protection? For example, is the protection contingent on the occurrence of specified events?

What are the fees and other costs? Products offering principal protection can be expensive. You should pay particular attention to the fees of any product you invest in, including those that offer principal protection. Ask your investment professional to explain all of the fees and costs associated with the investment.

How long will my money be tied up? Structured notes with principal protection are meant to be held to maturity and are often designed for long-term investors. If you need your money back early, you could pay a significant penalty. Furthermore, any downside protection offered might only kick in after a long lock-up period—or it might require you to hold the note until maturity.

Can I sell or liquidate before the maturity date? While it is easy to turn many investments into cash, liquid markets for some structured products might not exist. If you need to sell your structured note with principal protection before it matures, you might have to do it at a price less than the amount you paid for it, or you may not be able to sell it at all. This is true even if the product has a ticker symbol or has been approved for listing on an exchange.

Is there a call feature? If so, be sure you understand what can trigger the call and when is the earliest the investment may be called. You will also want to ask your investment professional what might be your game plan in the event your note gets called.

Are potential gains limited? Some structured notes with principal protection may have limits or caps on the gains you can earn based on the performance of the underlying asset, index or benchmark.

What are the tax implications? You might wish to consult with a tax advisor to understand the consequences of any particular investment, including imputed interest and any foreign tax consequences.

How does the pay-out structure work? Is it possible to lose money, or not have any gain at all, even if the underlying asset, index or benchmark goes up? Purchasing a structured note with principal protection does not guarantee positive returns. For example, the underlying asset, index or benchmark might not increase in value— or even if it does, there may be conditions, which in some cases can be counterintuitive, that limit your gains. And, if the entity backing the principal protection at maturity goes bankrupt, you could lose your entire principal.

What unique risks will I take on as a result of being exposed to the underlying asset, index or benchmark?

What is the credit risk of the note? Remember that any principal guarantee is subject to the creditworthiness of the guarantor, which is generally the securities firm that structures and issues the note. Be sure to find out as much as you can about the financial condition of the issuer and read its disclosures as carefully as you would for any other bond investment.

What other risks are associated with this particular product? Be sure you understand how the derivative component of the note impacts the pay-out structure—and ultimately your return.

What other investment choices are available to me? Carefully consider what might be a good fit for you, and whether there are alternatives to the product you are considering.

Even the simplest sounding products can be pretty complex. Always read a product's prospectus or disclosure statement carefully. If you can't understand how the product works, ask your investment professional for help. If you still can't understand the product, you should think twice about investing in it.

i. Additional Resources

FINRA Regulatory Notice 09-73
FINRA Alert, Principal-Protected Funds—
Security Has a Price
FINRA Smart Bond Investing
SEC Fast Answer, Equity-linked CDs

Section 18 - Target Date Funds

A number of companies offer "target date retirement funds," sometimes referred to as "target date funds" or "lifecycle funds." Target date funds, which are often mutual funds, hold a mix of stocks, bonds, and other investments. Over time, the mix gradually shifts according to the fund's investment strategy. Target date funds are designed to be long-term investments for individuals with particular retirement dates in mind. The name of the fund often refers to its target date. For example, you might see funds with names like "Portfolio 2030," "Retirement Fund 2030," or "Target 2030" that are designed for individuals who intend to retire in or near the year 2030.

Most target date funds are designed so that the fund's mix of investments will automatically change in a way that is intended to become more conservative as you approach the target date. Typically, the funds shift over time from a mix with a lot of stock investments in the beginning to a mix weighted more toward bonds. Target date funds are often available through 401(k) plans. Some 401(k) plans use these funds as the default investment for plan participants who have not selected their investments under the plan. Both before and after investing in a target date fund, consider carefully whether the fund is right for you.

Additional Information

Investor Bulletin: Target Date Retirement Funds

http://investor.gov/investing-basics/investment-products/target-date-funds

Section 19 - Investor Bulletin: Variable Annuities—An Introduction

02/06/2014

This SEC Office of Investor Education and Advocacy Investor Bulletin provides some basic facts about variable annuities and how they work. Variable annuities are complex products, and this Investor Bulletin focuses solely on the basics. For more in-depth information about variable annuities, see our companion publication, Variable Annuities: What You Should Know, available at www.sec.gov/investor/pubs/varannty.htm.

What is a variable annuity?

A variable annuity is an investment product with insurance features. It allows you to select from a menu of investment choices, typically mutual funds, within the variable annuity and, at a later date—such as retirement—allows you to receive a stream of payments over time. The value of your variable annuity will depend on how your investment choices perform.

What should I do before I invest in a variable annuity?

- **Know how they work.** Before you buy a variable annuity, know how it works, look up key terms you might not be familiar with, figure out how you'll be charged, and be prepared to ask your financial professional questions about whether the product is right for you.

- **Get the details—read the variable annuity prospectus.** Different products have different features. Ask your financial professional for the variable annuity prospectus, which will describe the product you're considering in detail. Read the prospectus carefully, and ask questions about what you don't understand. The prospectus—which should be available free of charge—contains important information about much of what's described in this Investor Bulletin, including charges, investment choices, death benefits, payout options, and other features.

- **Understand that they are not appropriate for short-term investors.** Variable annuities are long-term investments for retirement savings purposes and other long-range goals. They are not a good choice for short-term investing. If you take out your money too early from the variable annuity, substantial taxes and insurance company charges, among other things, may apply.

- **Realize that you could lose money**. Variable annuities involve investment risks, just like mutual funds do. If the investment choices you selected for the variable annuity perform poorly, you could lose money.

What's different about a variable annuity?

Although variable annuities usually are invested in mutual funds, they are different from mutual funds in important ways:

- **Variable annuities allow you to receive periodic payments**. A variable annuity allows you to receive **periodic payments** for the rest of your life or for the life of your spouse.

- **They offer a range of features, but be prepared to pay extra for them**. For example, most variable annuities offer a death benefit, which means that if you die before the insurer has started making payments to you, a person you have named as a beneficiary will receive a specified amount. But you'll pay for this feature during the time you own the product. Same with other features such as optional "riders," including so-called "guarantees," which are discussed in more detail below. Consider whether these features are right for you and are worth what you're paying for them.

- **Earnings are tax-deferred, but there are penalties for early withdrawal**. You pay no taxes on any income and investment gains on the investments that you hold in the variable annuity until you withdraw your money. But when you take your money out, you will be taxed on the earnings at **ordinary income tax rates** rather than at lower capital gains tax rates associated with other investments, like mutual funds. In addition, you may face a 10% federal income **tax penalty** if you withdraw the money before you are 59½ years old. Finally, if you're putting a variable annuity into a tax-advantaged account, like an IRA or other retirement account (*e.g.*, a 401(k) plan), you'll get no extra tax advantage.

> The tax rules that apply to variable annuities can be complicated—before investing, you may want to consult a tax adviser about the tax consequences to you of investing in a variable annuity.

How is my money in a variable annuity invested?

You allocate your payments (during what's called the "**accumulation phase**") to the investment choices available through the variable annuity. For example, you might direct 40% of your payments to a bond fund, 40% to a U.S. stock fund, and 20% to an international stock fund. The money you direct to each mutual fund investment choice will increase or decrease over time, depending on the mutual fund's performance. In addition, variable annuities often allow you to direct part of your purchase payments to a **fixed account run by the insurance company**. A fixed account, unlike a mutual fund, pays a fixed or minimum rate of interest.

Ask your financial professional for the prospectuses of the investment choices available through the variable annuity before you decide how to invest your money. Consider these important questions for each investment choice you are thinking about: (1) investment objectives, (2) fees and expenses, (3) risks and volatility, and (4) how the fund fits into your overall investment strategy.

How do I get my money out of the variable annuity?

When you begin to take money out of the variable annuity, that's called the "**payout phase**." At the beginning of the payout phase, you can elect to receive the value of your variable annuity all at once. Or, you can choose to receive a stream of payments—for example, for a period that you select (say, 20 years) or for a specified person's lifetime (such as your lifetime or the lifetime of you and your spouse).

What are living benefits?

Many variable annuities offer features designed to provide some protection from investment losses. These features are sometimes called "living benefits." They may also have names such as "guaranteed minimum income," "guaranteed minimum withdrawal," "guaranteed lifetime withdrawal," or "guaranteed minimum accumulation" benefits. Some such features provide that you will be able to receive a specified level of payments, regardless of the performance of your investment choices.

You pay extra for these features, so be sure what you choose is right for you, and worth what you're paying for it. Our variable annuity publication—*Variable Annuities: What You Should Know*—has more information about these features generally, and the product prospectus will have more information on how the particular living benefit you are considering works.

> ### *Caution!*
>
> You should consider the financial strength of the insurance company selling the variable annuity. This could affect the company's ability to meet its obligations to you under a living benefit, or to meet other obligations, such as a death benefit or a fixed account obligation.
>
> Living benefits are complex and often have limitations and conditions. For example:
>
> - You may be forced to select only certain investment choices, which may limit the return on your investment.
>
> - Withdrawals can reduce the amount that would otherwise be paid under the living benefit.

What will I pay to invest in a variable annuity?

You pay charges when you invest in a variable annuity. Be sure you understand all the charges before you invest.

These charges will reduce the value of your account and the return on your investment. Often, they will include:

- **Surrender charges**—Withdrawals made within a certain period after your purchase payment (usually within six to eight years, but sometimes 10 years or longer) will usually have a "surrender" charge deducted from the amount you withdraw.

- **Mortality and expense risk charge**— This charge is based on the value of your account—usually around 1.25% of the value of your account *per year*. It pays for the death benefit, and is sometimes used to pay the insurance company's costs to sell the contract—like commissions.

- **Investment option expenses**— Expenses for the investment choices you select.

- **Charges for other features**—Special features, such as a living benefit, an enhancement to the basic death benefit, or long-term care insurance, often cost extra.

Read the variable annuity prospectus and ask your financial professional to explain the charges that may apply. **We've highlighted some of the key ones here.**

What are tax-free exchanges?

Under U.S. tax law, you can exchange a variable annuity contract for a new annuity contract without paying any tax on any income and investment gains in your current variable annuity. These exchanges might be useful to you if you own a variable annuity but another annuity has features that you prefer, such as a larger death benefit, different annuity payout options, or different living benefits.

Exchanging your original variable annuity for a new one may have drawbacks. For example, when you surrender the old variable annuity, you may have to pay surrender charges. (Remember—exchanging your original variable annuity contract for a new annuity contract *generally is considered a withdrawal*.) Also, a new surrender charge period generally begins when you exchange into the new variable annuity. This means that, for a significant number of years, you typically will have to pay a surrender charge if you withdraw funds from the new variable annuity. In addition, features under the original contract, such as the death benefit and living benefits, might be better than you might have under the new contract. And the new variable annuity may have higher fees and charges than the old variable annuity, which will reduce your returns.

> ### *Caution!*
>
> Before you exchange one variable annuity product for another, compare both carefully.
>
> If you decide to do an exchange, you should first consult your financial professional or tax adviser to make sure that the exchange will be tax-free.
>
> See our variable annuity publication—Variable Annuities: What You Should Know—for more information about what you should think about, including a checklist of questions to ask yourself before you make your investment decision.

What are bonus credits?

Some insurance companies give you a credit that is added to your variable annuity contract value based on a percentage (typically from 1% to 5%) of your purchase payments. Sometimes the bonus is limited to money you put in initially or during the first year of owning the contract.

Ask questions before you invest—in anything

Don't be afraid to ask the financial professionals who are trying to sell you a variable annuity whether the product is right for you. Keep asking them questions until you are satisfied with their answers. And write down their answers, so there won't be any confusion later as to who said what.

Remember: Before purchasing a variable annuity, learn as much as possible about how it works, the benefits it provides, and the charges you will pay.

For More Information

Other SEC Online Resources (available at http://www.sec.gov)

Variable Annuities: What You Should Know— Contains more detailed information on topics like expenses, exchanges, tax treatment, and living benefits than what's in this bulletin.

Invest Wisely: An Introduction to Mutual Funds—Basic information about investing in mutual funds. Much of this information applies to variable annuities as well.

Mutual Fund Investing: Look at More Than a Fund's Past Performance—Describes some of the factors you should consider in choosing a mutual fund.

The Office of Investor Education and Advocacy has provided this information as a service to investors. It is neither a legal interpretation nor a statement of SEC policy. If you have questions concerning the meaning or application of a particular law or rule, please consult with an attorney who specializes in securities law.

http://investor.gov/news-alerts/investor-bulletins/investor-bulletin-variable-annuities-introduction [xxii]

Chapter 3 - Asset Allocation

Asset allocation involves dividing your investments among different assets, such as stocks, bonds, and cash. The asset allocation decision is a personal one. The allocation that works best for you changes at different times in your life, depending on how long you have to invest and your ability to tolerate risk.

Factors to consider include your:

Time Horizon. Your time horizon is the number of months, years, or decades you need to invest to achieve your financial goal. Investors with a longer time horizon may feel comfortable taking on riskier or more volatile investments. Those with a shorter time horizon may prefer to take on less risk.

Summary of Topics Covered:

a. What is diversification?
b. What is rebalancing?
c. What is Risk
d. Assessing Your Risk Tolerance

a. What is diversification?

The practice of spreading money among different investments to reduce risk is known as diversification. Diversification is a strategy that can be neatly summed up as "Don't put all your eggs in one basket."

One way to diversify is to allocate your investments among different kinds of assets. Historically, stocks, bonds, and cash have not moved up and down at the same time. Factors that may cause one asset class to perform poorly may improve returns for another asset class. People invest in various asset classes in the hope that if one is losing money, the others make up for those losses.

You'll also be better diversified if you spread your investments within each asset class. That means holding a number of different stocks or bonds, and investing in different industry sectors, such as consumer goods, health care, and technology. That way, if one sector is doing poorly, you may offset it with other holdings in sectors that are doing well.

Some investors find it easier to diversify by owning mutual funds. A mutual fund is a company that pools money from many investors and invests the money in stocks, bonds, and other financial products. Mutual funds make it easy for investors to own a small portion of many investments. A total stock market index fund, for example, owns stock in thousands of companies, providing a lot of diversification for one investment.

A mutual fund won't necessarily provide diversification, especially if it focuses on only one industry sector. If you invest in narrowly focused mutual funds, you may need to invest in several to be diversified. As you add more investments to your portfolio, you'll likely pay additional fees and expenses, which will lower your investment returns. So you'll need to consider these costs when deciding the best way to diversify your portfolio.

b. What is rebalancing?

Rebalancing is what investors do to bring their portfolio back to its original asset allocation mix. Rebalancing is needed because over time, some investments will grow faster than others. This may push your holdings out of alignment with your investment goals. By rebalancing, you will ensure that your portfolio does not overweight a particular asset category, and you'll return your portfolio to a comfortable level of risk.

For example, you might start with 60% of your portfolio invested in stocks, but see that rise to 80% due to market gains. To reestablish your original asset allocation mix, you'll either need to sell some of your stocks or invest in other asset categories.

There are three ways you can rebalance your portfolio:

1. You can sell investments where your holdings are over weighted and use the

proceeds to buy investments for underweighted asset categories.

2. You can buy new investments for underweighted asset categories.

3. If you are continuing to add to your investments, you can alter your contributions so that more goes to underweighted asset categories until your portfolio is back into balance.

Before you rebalance your portfolio, you should consider whether the method of rebalancing you decide to use would entail transaction fees or tax consequences. Your financial professional or tax adviser can help you identify ways that you can minimize these potential costs.

Some financial experts advise rebalancing at regular intervals, such as every six or 12 months. Others recommend rebalancing when your holdings of an asset class increase or decrease more than a certain pre-set percentage. In either case, rebalancing tends to work best when done on a relatively infrequent basis.

Shifting money away from an asset class when it is doing well in favor of an asset category that is doing poorly may not be easy. But it can be a wise move. By cutting back on current "winners" and adding more current "losers," rebalancing forces you to buy low and sell high.

http://investor.gov/investing-basics/guiding-principles/asset-allocation [xxiii]

Risk Tolerance. Risk tolerance is your ability and willingness to lose some or all of your original investment in exchange for potentially greater returns.

c. What is Risk?

All investments involve some degree of risk. In finance, risk refers to the degree of uncertainty and/or potential financial loss inherent in an investment decision. In general, as investment risks rise, investors seek higher returns to compensate themselves for taking such risks.

Every saving and investment product has different risks and returns. Differences include: how readily investors can get their money when they need it, how fast their money will grow, and how safe their money will be. In this section, we are going to talk about a number of risks investors face. They include:

Business Risk

With a stock, you are purchasing a piece of ownership in a company. With a bond, you are loaning money to a company. Returns from both of these investments require that that the company stays in business. If a company goes bankrupt and its assets are liquidated, common stockholders are the last in line to share in the proceeds. If there are assets, the company's bondholders will be paid first, then holders of preferred stock. If you are a common stockholder, you get whatever is left, which may be nothing.

If you are purchasing an annuity make sure you consider the financial strength of the insurance company issuing the annuity. You want to be sure that the company will still be around, and financially sound, during your payout phase.

Volatility Risk

Even when companies aren't in danger of failing, their stock price may fluctuate up or down. Large company stocks as a group, for example, have lost money on average about one out of every three years. Market fluctuations can be unnerving to some investors. A stock's price can be affected by factors inside the company, such as a faulty product, or by events the company has no control over, such as political or market events.

Inflation Risk

Inflation is a general upward movement of prices. Inflation reduces purchasing power, which is a risk for investors receiving a fixed rate of interest. The principal concern for individuals investing in cash equivalents is that inflation will erode returns.

Interest Rate Risk

Interest rate changes can affect a bond's value. If bonds are held to maturity the investor will receive the face value, plus interest. If sold before maturity, the bond may be worth more or less than the face value. Rising interest rates will make newly issued bonds more appealing to investors because the newer bonds will have a higher rate of interest than older ones. To sell an older bond with a lower interest rate, you might have to sell it at a discount.

Liquidity Risk

This refers to the risk that investors won't find a market for their securities, potentially preventing them from buying or selling when they want. This can be the case with the more complicated investment products. It may also be the case with products that charge a penalty for early withdrawal or liquidation such as a certificate of deposit (CD).

Are there any Guarantees?

The Federal Deposit Insurance Corporation (FDIC) – Savings accounts, insured money market accounts, and certificates of deposit (CDs) are generally viewed as safe because they are federally insured by FDIC. This independent agency of the federal government insures your money up to $250,000 per insured bank. It is important to note that the total is per depositor not per account. But there's a tradeoff between security and availability; your money earns a low interest rate.

The FDIC insures deposits only. It does not insure securities, mutual funds, or similar types of investments that banks and thrift institutions may offer.

The National Credit Union Administration (NCUA) –The National Credit Union Share Insurance Fund (NCUSIF) is the federal fund created by Congress in 1970 to insure credit union member's deposits in federally insured credit unions. The Dodd -Frank Act permanently established NCUA's standard maximum share insurance amount at $250,000. NCUSIF is backed by the full faith and credit of the U.S. Government.

Securities Investors Protection Corporation (SIPC) – Securities you own, including mutual funds that are held for your account by a broker, or a bank's brokerage subsidiary, are not insured against loss in value. The value of your investments can go up or down depending on the demand for them in the market. The Securities Investors Protection Corporation (SIPC), a non government entity, replaces missing stocks and other securities in customer accounts held by SIPC member firm up to $500,000, including up to $250,000 in cash, if the firm fails. For more information see www.sipc.org.

http://investor.gov/investing-basics/guiding-principles/what-is-risk xxiv

d. Assessing Your Risk Tolerance

When it comes to investing, risk and reward go hand in hand. The phrase "no pain, no gain" – comes close to summing up the relationship between risk and reward. Don't let anyone tell you otherwise: all investments involve some degree of risk. If you plan to buy securities – such as stocks, bonds, or mutual funds – it's important that you understand that you could lose some or all of the money you invest.

The reward for taking on risk is the potential for a greater investment return. If you have a financial goal with a long time horizon, you may make more money by carefully investing in higher risk assets, such as stocks or bonds, than if limit yourself to less risky assets. On the other hand, lower risk cash investments may be appropriate for short-term financial goals.

An aggressive investor, or one with a high risk tolerance, is willing to risk losing money to get potentially better results. A conservative investor, or one with a low risk tolerance, favors investments that maintain his or her original investment.

Many investment websites offer free online questionnaires to help you assess your risk tolerance. Some of the websites will even estimate asset allocations based on responses to the questionnaires. While the suggested asset allocations may be a useful starting point, keep in mind that the results may be biased towards financial products or services sold by companies or individuals sponsoring the websites.

http://investor.gov/investing-basics/guiding-principles/assessing-your-risk-tolerance [xxv]

Chapter Four - Avoiding Fraud

Don't be a fraud victim. A basic understanding of how scam artists work can help you to avoid fraud and protect your hard-earned money. Learning how to invest safely also can assist you in reaching your financial goals and will mean a huge difference in your retirement years. Here are some ways to help you avoid being scammed:

a. Learn what you can do to avoid investment fraud including red flags to watch for and where to go for help.

b. Learn how to protect yourself online, and how to protect your social media accounts.

c. Learn about the different types of investment fraud, including those found online and in social media.

Remember: if you have a question or concern about an investment, or you think you have encountered a fraud, please contact the SEC, FINRA, or your state securities regulator to report the fraud and to get assistance.

http://investor.gov/investing-basics/avoiding-fraud [xxvi]

a. What You Can Do to Avoid Investment Fraud

Ask questions. Fraudsters are counting on you not to investigate before you invest. Fend them off by doing your own digging. It's not enough to ask for more information or for references – fraudsters have no incentive to set you straight. Take the time to do your own independent research.

Research before you invest. Unsolicited emails, message board postings, and company news releases should never be used as the sole basis for your investment decisions. Understand a company's business and its products or services before investing. Look for the company's financial statements on the SEC's EDGAR filing system. You can also check out many investments by searching EDGAR.

Know the salesperson. Spend some time checking out the person touting the investment before you invest – even if you already know the person socially. Always find out whether the securities salespeople who contact you are licensed to sell securities in your state and whether they or their firms have had run-ins with regulators or other investors. You can check out the disciplinary history of brokers and advisers for free using the SEC's and FINRA's online databases. Your state securities regulator may have additional information.

Be wary of unsolicited offers. Be especially careful if you receive an unsolicited pitch to invest in a company, or see it praised online, but can't find current financial information about it from independent sources. It could be a "pump and dump" scheme. Be wary if someone recommends foreign or "off-shore" investments. If something goes wrong, it's harder to find out what happened and to locate money sent abroad.

Protect yourself online. Online and social marketing sites offer a wealth of opportunity for fraudsters. For tips on how to protect yourself online see Protect Your Social Media Accounts.

Know what to look for. Make yourself knowledgeable about different types of fraud and red flags that may signal investment fraud.

Red flags for fraud and common persuasion tactics

How do successful, financially intelligent people fall prey to investment fraud? Researchers have found that investment fraudsters hit their targets with an array of persuasion techniques that are tailored to the victim's psychological profile. Here are red flags to look for:

If it sounds too good to be true, it is. Watch for "phantom riches." Compare promised yields with current returns on well-known stock indexes. Any investment opportunity that claims you'll receive substantially more could be highly risky – and that means you might lose money. Be careful of claims that an investment will make "*incredible gains,*" is a "*breakout stock pick*" or has "*huge upside and almost no risk!*" Claims like these are hallmarks of extreme risk or outright fraud.

"Guaranteed returns" aren't. Every investment carries some degree of risk, which is reflected in the rate of return you can expect to receive. If your money is perfectly safe, you'll most likely get a low return. High returns entail high risks, possibly including a total loss on the investments. Most fraudsters spend a lot of time trying to convince investors that extremely high returns are "guaranteed" or "can't miss." They try to plant an image in your head of what your life will be like when you are rich. Don't believe it.

Beware the "halo" effect. Investors can be blinded by a "halo" effect when a con artist comes across as likeable or trustworthy. Credibility can be faked. Check out actual qualifications.

"Everyone is buying it." Watch out for pitches that stress how "everyone is investing in this, so you should, too." Think about whether you are interested in the product. If a sales presentation focuses on how many others have bought the product, this could be a red flag.

Pressure to send money RIGHT NOW. Scam artists often tell their victims that this is a once-in-a-lifetime offer and it will be gone tomorrow. But resist the pressure to invest quickly and take the time you need to investigate before sending money.

Reciprocity. Fraudsters often try to lure investors through free investment seminars, figuring if they do a small favor for you, such as supplying a free lunch, you will do a big favor for them and invest in their product. There is never a reason to make a quick decision on an investment. If you attend a free lunch, take the material home and research both the investment and the individual selling it before you invest. Always make sure the product is right for you and that you understand what you are buying and all the associated fees.

Where can I go for help?

If you have a question or concern about an investment, or you think you have encountered one of these frauds, please contact the SEC, FINRA, or your state securities regulator to report the fraud and to get assistance.

U.S. Securities and Exchange Commission
Office of Investor Education and Advocacy
100 F Street, NE
Washington, DC 20549-0213
Telephone: (800) 732-0330
Fax: (202) 772-9295

Financial Industry Regulatory Authority (FINRA)
FINRA Complaints and Tips
9509 Key West Avenue
Rockville, MD 20850
Telephone: (301) 590-6500
Fax: (866) 397-3290

North American Securities Administrators Association (NASAA)
750 First Street NE
Suite 1140
Washington, DC 20002
Telephone: (202) 737-0900
Fax: (202) 783-3571

http://investor.gov/investing-basics/avoiding-fraud/what-you-can-do-avoid-investment-fraud xxvii

b. Protect Your Social Media Accounts

The Internet has made our lives easier in so many ways. However, you need to know how you can protect your privacy and avoid fraud. Remember, not only can people be defrauded when using the Internet for investing; the fraudsters use information online to send bogus materials, solicit or phish.

Phishing is the attempt to obtain financial or confidential information from Internet users. This phishing expedition usually begins with an email that looks as if it is from a legitimate source, often a financial institution. The email contains a link to a fake website that looks like the real site. Fraudsters want you to provide account and password information, and then they have access to your account.

Here's what you can do to protect yourself when using social media:

Privacy Settings: Always check the default privacy settings when opening an account on a social media website. The default privacy settings on many social media websites are typically broad and may permit sharing of information to a vast online community. Modify the setting, if appropriate, before posting any information on a social media website.

Biographical Information: Many social media websites require biographical information to open an account. You can limit the information made available to other social media users. Consider customizing your privacy settings to minimize the amount of biographical information others can view on the website.

Account Information: Never give account information, Social Security numbers, bank information or other sensitive financial information on a social media website. If you need to speak to a financial professional, use a firm-sponsored method of communication, such as telephone, letter, firm e-mail or firm-sponsored website.

Friends/Contacts: When choosing friends or contacts on a social media site, think about why you use the website. Decide whether it is appropriate to accept a "friend" or other membership request from a financial service provider, such as a financial adviser or broker-dealer. There is no obligation to accept a "friend" request of a service provider or anyone you do not know or do not know well.

Site Features: Familiarize yourself with the functionality of the social media website before broadcasting messages on the site. Who will be able to see your messages -- only specified recipients, or all users?

On-Line Security Tips

As with all computer and web-based accounts, take precautions to keep your social media account information secure. Here are some security tips:

- Pick a "strong" password, keep it secure, and change it frequently.

- Use different passwords for different accounts.

- Use caution with public computers or wireless connections. Try to avoid accessing your social media accounts on public or other shared computers. But if you must do so, remember to log out completely by clicking the "log out" button on the social media website to terminate the online session.

- Be mindful of accessing your social media accounts on public wireless connections, such as at a coffee shop or airport. It is very easy to eavesdrop on Internet traffic, including passwords and other sensitive data, on a public wireless network.

- Be extra careful before clicking on links sent to you, even if by a friend.

- Secure your mobile devices. If your mobile devices are linked to your social media accounts, make sure that these devices are password protected in case they are lost or stolen.

http://investor.gov/investing-basics/avoiding-fraud/protect-your-social-media-accounts xxviii

c. Types of Fraud

Securities frauds come in many types and varieties. Whether you are a first-time investor or have been investing for many years, here are some basic facts you should know about the different types of fraud.

1. Advance Fee Fraud
2. Affinity Fraud
3. High Yield Investment Programs
4. Internet and Social Media Fraud
5. Microcap Fraud
6. Ponzi Schemes
7. Pre-IPO Investment Scams
8. Pyramid Scheme
9. "Prime Bank" Investments
10. Promissory Notes
11. Pump and Dump Schemes
12. Commodity Pool Fraud
13. Commodity Pool Fraud
14. Precious Metals Fraud

1. Advance Fee Fraud

Advance fee frauds ask for payment up front before the deal can go through. The advance payment may be described as a fee, tax, commission, or incidental expense that will be repaid later. Some advance fee schemes target investors who already purchased underperforming securities and offer to sell those securities if an "advance fee" is paid.

One example is the so-called Nigerian advance fee fraud, where someone pretending to be a Nigerian official or businessperson promises high profits for help moving money out of Nigeria. This scam is so prevalent that the U.S. Secret Service has a task force devoted to it.

Other advance fee frauds try to fool investors with official-sounding websites and e-mail addresses. These addresses may contain ".gov" and end in ".us" or ".org." U.S. government agency websites or e-mail addresses end in ".gov," ".mil," or "fed.us." Be wary of a website or correspondence claiming to be from a U.S. government agency whose e-mail address does not end in ".gov", ".mil", or "fed.us".

2. Affinity Fraud

Affinity frauds target members of identifiable groups, such as the elderly, or religious or ethnic communities. The fraudsters involved in affinity scams often are – or pretend to be – members of the group. They may enlist respected leaders from the group to spread the word about the scheme, convincing them it is legitimate and worthwhile. Many times, those leaders become unwitting victims of the fraud they helped to promote.

These scams exploit the trust and friendship that exists in groups of people. Because of the tight-knit structure of many groups, outsiders may not know about the affinity scam. Victims may try to work things out within the group rather than notify authorities or pursue legal remedies.

Affinity scams often involve "Ponzi" or pyramid schemes where new investor money is used to pay earlier investors, making it appear as if the investment is successful and legitimate.

http://investor.gov/investing-basics/avoiding-fraud/types-fraud/affinity-fraud [xxix]

3. High Yield Investment Programs

The Internet is awash in so-called "high-yield investment programs" or "HYIPs." These are unregistered investments typically run by unlicensed individuals – and they are often frauds. The hallmark of an HYIP scam is the promise of incredible returns at little or no risk to the investor. A HYIP website might promise annual (or even monthly, weekly, or daily!) returns of 30 or 40 percent – or more. Some of these scams may use the term "prime bank" program. ***If you are approached online to invest in one of these, you should exercise extreme caution - it is likely a fraud.***

http://investor.gov/investing-basics/avoiding-fraud/types-fraud/high-yield-investment-programs[xxx]

4. Internet and Social Media Fraud

Many investors use the Internet and social media to help them with investment decisions. While these online tools can provide many benefits for investors, these same tools can make attractive targets for criminals. Criminals are quick to adapt to new technologies – and the Internet is no exception.

The Internet is a useful way to reach a mass audience without spending a lot of time or money. A website, online message, or social media site can reach large numbers with minimum effort. It's easy for fraudsters to make their messages look real and credible and sometimes hard for investors to tell the difference between fact and fiction. That's why you should think twice before you invest your money in any opportunity you find online.

The key to avoiding investment fraud on social media sites or elsewhere on the Internet is to be an educated investor. To learn specific steps you can take, see What You Can Do to Avoid Investment Fraud. Below, we tell you where various types of fraud may show up online such as Social media, Online investment newsletters, Online bulletin boards and chat rooms and Spam.

Social media

Social media, such as Facebook, YouTube, Twitter, and LinkedIn, have become key tools for U.S. investors. Whether they are seeking research on particular stocks, background information on a broker-dealer or investment adviser, guidance on an overall investment strategy, up to date news or to simply want to discuss the markets with others, investors turn to social media. Social media also offers a number of features that criminals may find attractive. Fraudsters can use social media in their efforts to appear legitimate, to hide behind anonymity, and to reach many people at low cost. For additional information, see these Investor Alerts and Bulletins:

Investor Alert: Social Media and Investing - Avoiding Fraud
Investor Bulletin: Social Media and Investing – Understanding Your Accounts

Always be wary of unsolicited offers to invest.
Unsolicited sales pitches may be part of a
fraudulent investment scheme. If you receive
an unsolicited message from someone you
don't know containing a "can't miss"
investment, your best move maybe to pass up
the "opportunity" and report it to the SEC
Complaint Center.

Online investment newsletters

While legitimate online newsletters contain
valuable information, others are tools for
fraud. Some companies pay online newsletters
to "tout" or recommend their stocks. Touting
isn't illegal as long as the newsletters disclose
who paid them, how much they're getting paid,
and the form of the payment, usually cash or
stock. But fraudsters often lie about the
payments they receive and their track records.

Fraudulent promoters may claim to offer
independent, unbiased recommendations in
newsletters when they stand to profit from
convincing others to buy or sell certain stocks.
They may spread false information to promote
worthless stocks.

The fact that these so-called "newsletters" may
be advertised on legitimate websites, including
on the online financial pages of news

organizations, does not mean that they are not fraudulent.

Online bulletin boards and chat rooms

Online bulletin boards, chat rooms and social media sites are a way for investors to share information. While some messages may be true, many turn out to be bogus – or even scams. Fraudsters may use online discussions to pump up a company or pretend to reveal "inside" information about upcoming announcements, new products, or lucrative contracts.

You never know for certain who you're dealing with, or whether they're credible, because many sites allow users to hide their identity behind multiple aliases. People claiming to be unbiased observers may actually be insiders, large shareholders, or paid promoters. One person can easily create the illusion of widespread interest in a small, thinly traded stock by posting numerous messages under various aliases.

Other online offerings may not be fraudulent *per se*, but may nonetheless fail to comply with the applicable registration provisions of the federal securities laws. While the federal securities laws require the registration of solicitations or "offerings," some offerings are exempt. *Always determine if a securities offering is registered with the SEC or a state, or is otherwise exempt from registration, before investing.*

Spam

"Spam" – junk e-mail – often is used to promote bogus investment schemes or to spread false information about a company. With a bulk e-mail program, spammers can send personalized messages to millions of people at once for much less than the cost of cold calling or traditional mail. Many scams, including advance fee frauds, use spam to reach potential victims.

Many of the frauds that show up on social media are not unique to the Internet. These frauds range from "pump and dump" schemes to promises of "guaranteed returns," from "High Yield Investment Programs" to affinity fraud.

http://investor.gov/investing-basics/avoiding-fraud/types-fraud/internet-social-media-fraud
xxxi

5. Microcap Fraud

Information is the investor's best tool when it comes to investing wisely. It may be difficult to find accurate information about microcap stocks (*i.e.,* low-priced stocks issued by the smallest of companies), including penny stocks (*i.e.,* the very lowest priced stocks). Many microcap companies do not file financial reports with the SEC, so it can be hard for investors to get the facts about the company's management, products, services, and finances. When publicly-available information is scarce, fraudsters can easily spread false information about microcap companies, making profits for themselves while creating losses for unsuspecting investors. **Here's how some fraudsters disseminate false information about microcap companies:**

- **Paid Promoters.** Some microcap companies pay stock promoters to recommend or "tout" the microcap stock in supposedly independent and unbiased investment newsletters, research reports, or radio and television shows. Paid promoters are often behind the unsolicited "junk" faxes, e-mail messages, online advertisements or high-end glossy mailers you may receive touting a microcap or penny stock company. The federal securities laws require the publications to disclose who paid them for the promotion, the amount, and the type of payment. But many fraudsters fail to do so and mislead investors into believing that they are receiving independent advice.

- **Internet Fraud.** Fraudsters often use aliases on Internet bulletin boards and chat rooms to hide their identities and post messages urging investors to buy stock in microcap companies based on supposedly "inside" information about impending developments at the companies. For more information about Internet fraud and on-line investing, read Internet Fraud and Tips for Online Investing: What You Need to Know About Trading in Fast-Moving Markets.

- **Email Spam.** Fraudsters distribute junk e-mail or "spam" over the Internet to spread false information quickly and cheaply about a microcap company to potential investors. Spam allows the unscrupulous to target many more potential investors than cold calling or mass mailing.

- **"Boiler Rooms" and Cold Calling.** Dishonest brokers set up "boiler rooms" where a small army of high-pressure salespeople use banks of telephones to make cold calls to as many potential investors as possible. These strangers hound investors to buy "house stocks" - stocks that the firm buys or sells as a market maker or has in its inventory. To learn more about cold calling, read Cold Calling - Know Your Rights.

- **Questionable Press Releases.**
  Fraudsters often issue press releases
  that contain exaggerations or lies about
  the microcap company's sales,
  acquisitions, revenue projections, or new
  products or services. These fraudulent
  press releases are sometimes then
  disseminated through legitimate financial
  news portals on the Internet.

*If you are considering investing in a
microcap company, watch out for these
"Red Flags":*

- SEC Trading Suspensions

- E-mail and Fax Spam

- Assets are Large but Revenues are Small

- Odd Items in the Footnotes of Financial
  Statements

- Unusual Auditing Issues

- Insiders Own Large Amounts of Stock

Even in the absence of fraud, microcap stocks
historically have been more volatile and less
liquid than the stock of larger companies. *To
invest wisely and avoid investment scams,
research each investment opportunity
thoroughly and ask questions:*

- Find out whether the company has registered its securities with the SEC or your state securities regulator.

- Make sure you understand the company's business and its products or services.

- Read carefully the most recent reports the company has filed with the SEC and pay attention to the company's financial statements, particularly if they are not audited or not certified by an accountant. If the company does not file reports with the SEC, be sure to ask your broker for what's called the "Rule 15c2-11 file" on the company.

- Check out the people running the company with your state securities regulator, and find out if they've ever made money for investors before. Also ask whether the people running the company have had run-ins with the regulators or other investors.

- Make sure the broker and his or her firm are registered with the SEC, and licensed or registered to do business in your state. If the broker or firm is not registered, do not trade with them. Visit FINRA's BrokerCheck website or call FINRA's toll-free BrokerCheck hotline at (800) 289-9999, to determine whether the broker or firm is registered with the SEC, and to check whether there is a history of investor complaints or problems with regulators. Also contact your state securities regulator to determine whether the broker or firm is licensed or registered with your state securities regulator to do business with you, and ask about any complaints.

http://investor.gov/investing-basics/avoiding-fraud/types-fraud/microcap-fraud

6. Ponzi Scheme

A Ponzi scheme is an investment fraud that pays existing investors with funds collected from new investors. Ponzi scheme organizers often promise to invest your money and generate high returns with little or no risk. But in many Ponzi schemes, the fraudsters do not invest the money. Instead, they use it to pay those who invested earlier and may keep some for themselves.

With little or no legitimate earnings, Ponzi schemes require a constant flow of new money to survive. When it becomes hard to recruit new investors, or when large numbers of existing investors cash out, these schemes tend to collapse.

Ponzi schemes are named after Charles Ponzi, who duped investors in the 1920s with a postage stamp speculation scheme.

Ponzi scheme "red flags"

Many Ponzi schemes share common characteristics. Look for these warning signs:

- **High returns with little or no risk.** Every investment carries some degree of risk, and investments yielding higher returns typically involve more risk. Be highly suspicious of any "guaranteed" investment opportunity.

- **Overly consistent returns.** Investments tend to go up and down over time. Be skeptical about an investment that regularly generates positive returns regardless of overall market conditions.

- **Unregistered investments.** Ponzi schemes typically involve investments that are not registered with the SEC or with state regulators. Registration is important because it provides investors with access to information about the company's management, products, services, and finances.

- **Unlicensed sellers.** Federal and state securities laws require investment professionals and firms to be licensed or registered. Most Ponzi schemes involve unlicensed individuals or unregistered firms.

- **Secretive, complex strategies.** Avoid investments if you don't understand them or can't get complete information about them.

- **Issues with paperwork.** Account statement errors may be a sign that funds are not being invested as promised.

- **Difficulty receiving payments.** Be suspicious if you don't receive a payment or have difficulty cashing out. Ponzi scheme promoters sometimes try to prevent participants from cashing out by offering even higher returns for staying put.

http://investor.gov/investing-basics/avoiding-fraud/types-fraud/ponzi-scheme [xxxii]

7. Pre-IPO Investment Scams

The SEC's Office of Investor Education and Advocacy has issued an updated Investor Alert to warn investors about investment scams that purport to offer investors the opportunity to buy pre-IPO shares of companies, including social media and technology companies such as Facebook and Twitter. SEC staff is aware of a number of complaints and inquiries about these types of frauds, which may be promoted on social media and internet sites, by telephone, email, in person, or by other means.

http://investor.gov/investing-basics/avoiding-fraud/types-fraud/pre-ipo-investment-scams
xxxiii

8. Pyramid Scheme

In the classic "pyramid" scheme, participants attempt to make money solely by recruiting new participants. The hallmark of these schemes is the promise of sky-high returns in a short period of time.

Pyramid scheme promoters may go to great lengths to make the program look like a multi-level marketing program selling legitimate products or services. But these fraudsters use money from new recruits to pay off early stage investors until eventually, the pyramid collapses. At some point, the schemes get too big, the promoter cannot raise enough money from new investors to pay earlier investors, and people lose their money.

Ponzi and pyramid schemes are closely related because they both involve paying longer-standing members with money from new participants, instead of actual profits from investing or selling products to the public. Here is how to tell them apart:

	Pyramid Scheme	Ponzi Scheme
Typical "hook"	Earn high profits by making one payment and finding others to become distributors of a product. The scheme typically does not involve a genuine product. The purported product may not exist or it may be "sold" only to other people who	Earn high investment returns with little or no risk by simply handing over your money; often the investment does not exist or only a small percentage of incoming funds are actually invested.

	also become distributors.	
Payments	Must pay a one-time or recurring participation fee and recruit new distributors to receive payments.	No recruiting necessary to receive payments.
Interaction with original promoter	Sometimes none. New participants may enter the pyramid scheme at different levels.	Promoter generally interacts directly with all participants.
How the scheme works	Funds from new participants are used to pay recruiting commissions to earlier participants.	Funds from new investors are used to pay purported returns to earlier investors.

Collapse	Fast. An exponential increase in the number of participants is required at each level.	May be relatively slow if existing participants reinvest money.

http://investor.gov/investing-basics/avoiding-fraud/types-fraud/pyramid-scheme xxxiv

9. "Prime Bank" Investments

If someone approaches you about investing in a so-called "Prime Bank" program, "Prime World Bank" financial instrument, or similar high-yield security, you should know that these investments do not exist. They are all scams.

Prime Bank programs often claim investors' funds will be used to buy and trade "Prime Bank" instruments. Promoters make the schemes seem legitimate, using complex, sophisticated and official-sounding terms. The investment may be described as debentures, standby letters of credit, bank guarantees, an offshore trading program, a high-yield investment program, or some variation.

To reassure investors, promoters may claim that the instrument is issued, traded, or guaranteed by a well-known organization such as the World Bank, the International Monetary Fund(IMF), a central bank, such as the U.S. Federal Reserve, or the International Chamber of Commerce (ICC).

Secrecy is another tip-off. Prime Bank scheme promoters frequently claim that investment opportunities of this type are by invitation only and limited to select, wealthy customers. They cite secrecy if potential investors ask for references, and sometimes ask investors to sign non-disclosure agreements.

Some promoters are audacious enough to advertise in national newspapers. They may avoid using the term "Prime Bank note," and tell prospective investors that their programs do not involve Prime Bank instruments. Regardless of what they're called, the basic pitch remains the same, and investors should remain vigilant against offers to invest in high-yield, risk-free international finance programs.

http://investor.gov/investing-basics/avoiding-fraud/types-fraud/prime-bank-investments [xxxv]

10. Promissory Notes

Promissory notes are a form of debt that companies sometimes use to raise money. They typically involve investors loaning money to a company in exchange for a fixed amount of periodic income. Although promissory notes can be appropriate investments for many individuals, some fraudsters use promissory notes to defraud investors, especially the elderly.

For tips on how to avoid promissory note scams, read Broken Promises: Promissory Note Fraud. For more information, the Financial Industry Regulatory Authority (FINRA) website has an alert on Promissory Notes Can Be Less Than Promised.

http://investor.gov/investing-basics/avoiding-fraud/types-fraud/promissory-notes [xxxvi]

11. Pump and Dump Schemes

"Pump and dump" schemes have two parts. In the first, promoters try to boost the price of a stock with false or misleading statements about the company. Once the stock price has been pumped up, fraudsters move on to the second part, where they seek to profit by selling their own holdings of the stock, dumping shares into the market.

These schemes often occur on the Internet where it is common to see messages urging readers to buy a stock quickly. Often, the promoters will claim to have "inside" information about a development that will be positive for the stock. After these fraudsters dump their shares and stop hyping the stock, the price typically falls, and investors lose their money.

http://investor.gov/investing-basics/avoiding-fraud/types-fraud/pump-dump-schemes [xxxvii]

12. Commodity Pool Fraud

The following information is designed to warn you about a type of fraud that involves individuals and firms, often unregistered, offering investments in commodity pools. In these fraudulent schemes, your money is misused (often spent on improper expenses). The pool operators advertise based on false claims of high profits and low risk.

Signs of a Possible Fraudulent Sales Pitch

- Lead you to believe you can profit from current news already known to the public.
  "As a result of that hurricane, the price of oil futures will increase substantially."

- Made through word of mouth referrals or emails from friends, relatives, members of churches or social groups – one fraudulent pool operator even solicited his cancer support group.

- Claims to know unique market trends or to have a record of highly profitable trading.

- Promises quick, large and guaranteed returns.

- Contacts you asking for personal information such as your full name, phone number, email or home address.

- Requests cash immediately.

Possible Persuasion Tactics You May Experience

- Dangling the prospect of wealth and enticing you with something you want, but can't have.
  "This gold purchase is guaranteed to double in three months!"

- Trying to build credibility by claiming to be with a reputable firm or to have a special credential or experience.
  "Believe me, as a senior vice president of EZY Money Inc., I would never sell an investment that doesn't produce."

- Leading you to believe that other savvy investors have already invested.

"This is how Bob got his start. I know it's a lot of money, but I'm in—and so are my mom and half her club—and it's worth every dime."

- Offering to do a small favor for you in return for a big favor.
  "I'll give you a break on my commission if you buy now—half off."

- Creating a false sense of urgency by claiming limited supply.
  "There are only two units left, so I'd sign up today if I were you."

Before Investing in a Commodity Pool, Ask, Ask, and Ask Some More!!

- Contact the CFTC at 866.366.2382 or the **National Futures Association** to check the company's registration status, business background, and disciplinary history.

- Ask for copies of the account statements that registered trading firms provide to the pool operator.

- Ask to see the commodity pool's risk disclosure documents and performance history.

- Ask about all fees and commissions charged by the commodity pool operator.

- Ask how the financial professional is qualified to provide you with this service.

- Ask how the product meets your financial needs.

If you have questions, are aware of suspicious activities, or believe you have been defrauded, please let the CFTC know quickly.

http://www.cftc.gov/ConsumerProtection/FraudAwarenessPrevention/CFTCFraudAdvisories/fraudadv_commoditypool [xxxviii]

13. Foreign Currency Trading (Forex) Fraud

The Forex market is volatile and carries substantial risks. It is **not** the place to put any money that you cannot afford to lose, such as retirement funds, as you can lose most or all it very quickly. The CFTC has witnessed a sharp rise in Forex trading scams in recent years and wants to advise you on how to identify potential fraud.

Signs of a Possible Fraudulent Sales Pitch

- Lead you to believe you can profit from current news already known to the public.

- Made through word of mouth referrals or emails from friends and relatives, members of community organizations, churches, or social groups.

- Contacts you asking for personal information such as your name, phone number, and email and home addresses.

- Promising that with Forex there is no "down-turning market".

Possible Persuasion Tactics You May Experience

- Dangling the prospect of wealth and enticing you with something you want, but can't have. "This Euro/dollar deal is guaranteed to rise double what your current investments are doing."

- Trying to build credibility by claiming to be with a reputable firm or to have a special credential or experience. "Believe me, as a 10-year senior vice president at this firm, I would never sell something that doesn't produce."

- Leading you to believe that other savvy people have already invested.
  "This is how Bob down the street from you got his start. I know it's a lot of money, but I'm in—and so is half our club. It's worth every dime."

- Offering to do a small favor for you in return for a big favor.
  "I'll give you a break on my normal Forex commission if you buy now—half off."

- Creating a false sense of urgency by claiming limited supply.
  "There are only two units left and the Asian market is about to open, so I'd sign up today."

Watch for These Red Flags to Help Identify Foreign Currency Trading Scams

- Promises that with Forex, there is no "bear" market

- Firms that claim you can or should trade in the interbank market

- Requests to send or transfer cash quickly via the Internet, by mail, or otherwise

- Difficulty getting background information about the person and/or company

Before Participating in Forex Trading, Ask, Ask, and Ask Some More!!

- Contact the CFTC to check the company's registration status, business background, and disciplinary history

- Ask about the details of the Forex trading market and your obligations if you participate

- Ask about the firm and the individual's performance record on behalf of other clients

- Ask anyone not willing to comply why they are being hesitant to do so

- Ask for all information in writing. Do not rely on oral promises or statements

- Check all information you receive to ensure that the company is and does what it says it does

- Ask for a written risk disclosure statement

- Ask for the advice of an independent and licensed financial advisor or consultant whom you trust

Questions to Ask any Financial Professional

- How are you qualified to provide me this service?

- How does this product meet my financial needs?

- How are you paid for your service?

If You Decide to Participate In Forex Trading

- Do not deposit more funds than you can afford to lose.

- Do not mortgage your home or cash in your savings.

- Do not trade on margin unless you understand it. Margin trading can make you responsible for losses that greatly exceed the dollar amount you deposited.

If you have questions, are aware of suspicious activities, or believe you have been defrauded, please contact the CFTC quickly. Call the CFTC at 866.366.2382 or file a **tip or complaint**.

http://www.cftc.gov/ConsumerProtection/Frau dAwarenessPrevention/CFTCFraudAdvisories/fr audadv_forex [xxxix]

14. Precious Metals Fraud

The following information is designed to notify you about tricky promises of easy profits from rising prices in precious metals such as gold, silver, palladium, and platinum. Below is information about these offers and simple ways to spot offers that could be scams.

Signs of a Possible Fraudulent Sales Pitch

- Lead you to believe you can profit from current news already known to the public.
  "Since that mine disaster, you are certain to earn big returns on your deposit."

- Made by people who call themselves "metals dealers" or "merchants".

- Advertised on radio, television, or online.

- Contacts you asking for personal information such as your name, phone number, and email and home address.

- Calls received from a broker or salesman from the company to promote the precious metals purchase.

Possible Persuasion Tactics You May Experience

- Dangling the prospect of wealth and enticing you with something you want, but can't have.
  "This gold purchase is guaranteed to rise double what your current investments are doing."

- Trying to build credibility by claiming to be with a reputable firm or to have a special credential or experience.
  "Believe me, as a senior vice president of XYZ Metals Merchant Inc., I would never sell an investment that doesn't produce."

- Leading you to believe that other savvy investors have already invested.
  "This is how Bob down your street got his start. I know it's a lot of money, but I'm in and so is half our club."

- Offering to do a small favor for you in return for a big favor.
  "I'll give you a break on my commission if you buy now—half off."

- Creating a false sense of urgency by claiming limited supply.
  "There are only two units left and the Asian market is about to open, so I'd sign up today."

Frequent Sales Arrangement That May Indicate Problems

- Claiming you can make a lot of money with little risk by purchasing through a "financing agreement".

- Structured so you only pay a small percentage (between 15% and 25%) of the total purchase price.

- Full price paid by a loan, that the company arranges, to finance the rest of your purchase.

- Claims that the company will store the precious metals for you in a storage facility or "bank".

Frequent Problems

- Often do not use your money to purchase metals at any time.

- Do not actually arrange for loan financing with an independent financial institution, but charge phony interest.

- Do not store metal with an independent bank or storage facility, but charge storage fees.

- Fraudulently fail to point out that because you are not paying the full price for the metals, you will have to send the company additional funds if prices move unfavorably.

- Often use your funds to pay themselves commissions, leaving little for you.

- Usually do not make you the promised profits and lose all or a significant portion of your money.

o. Precious Metals Sales Warning Signs!

- States that precious metals transactions are not regulated by the CFTC or the National Futures Association.

- Agreement that does not identify the financial institution or bank that will be loaning the you money.

- Agreement that does not identify where the physical metal is located.

- Claims to deliver the physical metal to an overseas storage facility.

- Difficulty in verifying the company's license.

- A salesperson that cannot provide a way to prove their licensure from a government agency.

- A salesperson offering highly complex purchasing techniques for unusual success.

- Missing documentation that seems necessary.

Before Investing in Precious Metals, Ask, Ask, and Ask Some More!

- Contact the CFTC at 866.366.2382 or the **National Futures Association** to check the company's registration status, business background, and disciplinary history.

- Ask how the financial professional is qualified to provide you with this service.

- Ask how the product meets your financial needs.

- Ask how the financial professional is paid for his/her service.

If you have questions, are aware of suspicious activities, or believe you have been defrauded, please contact the CFTC quickly. Call the CFTC or file a tip or complaint.

http://www.cftc.gov/ConsumerProtection/FraudAwarenessPrevention/CFTCFraudAdvisories/fraudadv_preciousmetals [xl]

Chapter 5 - Cold Calling – Know Your Rights

The telephone rings as you're sitting down to dinner or putting the kids to bed. A stranger is selling something. It's known as "cold calling." For many businesses, including securities firms, cold calling serves as a legitimate way to reach potential customers. But sometimes serious trouble and financial losses await you at the other end of the line. You may be pressured to buy a bad investment. Or the investment might be a scam.

Whether the calls are annoying, abusive, or downright crooked, you *can* stop cold callers. This Alert tells you how to stop cold calls, what your legal rights are, which red flags to avoid, and how to evaluate any investment opportunity that comes your way over the telephone.

Use the "National Do Not Call Registry" to Reduce Unwanted Cold Calls

The National Do Not Call Registry was jointly established by the Federal Trade Commission and the Federal Communications Commission to give Americans a way to avoid getting telemarketing calls at home. Adding your home or cell phone number to the Registry is easy — and absolutely free. You may register two ways:

1. **Online** at donotcall.gov, as long as you have a working email address. Shortly after you sign up, you will receive an email confirmation from donotcall.gov that contains a link you must click to complete the process. If you do not click on this link within 72 hours, your phone number will not be registered.

2. **Over the telephone** by calling toll-free **1-888-382-1222** from the number you wish to register.

Your number will remain on the Registry for five years — or sooner if you decide to terminate your phone service or take your number off the Registry.

Tip: Be sure to sign up for the National Do Not Call registry every five years. Your registration will expire five years from the day you register, so you'll need to place your number back in the Registry after the expiration date to limit cold calls.

Be aware that putting your home phone or cell phone numbers on the National Do Not Call Registry will not stop all telemarketing calls. You still may receive calls from:

Political organizations, charities, and telephone surveyors.

Companies with whom you have an established business relationship. Under FINRA rules, an established business relationship includes making a financial transaction or having a security position, money balance or account activity with the firm within the past 18 months. A securities representative may also call you for up to three months after you've contacted the firm to ask about a product or service.

Companies you have provided express written permission to make telephone contact.

If the caller is a family member, friend, or acquaintance, they also may still call you.

Understand Your Rights

When telemarketers, including people from the securities industry, call to sell you something, they must follow these important rules:

Cold Callers Must Check the "National Do Not Call Registry" — With very few exceptions, federal law requires all telemarketers, including securities firms, to search the National Do Not Call Registry every 31 days to avoid calling any numbers that are on the Registry.

Tip: If your number has been on the Registry for 31 days and you receive a cold call from an entity that doesn't meet any of the exceptions to the cold calling rules, you can file a complaint at donotcall.gov or by calling toll-free 1-888-382-1222. You'll need to know the date of the call and the company's name or phone number to file a complaint.

Cold Callers May Call You at Home Only Between 8:00 a.m. and 9:00 p.m. — These time restrictions for calls at home apply *unless* you have an established business relationship with the firm or you gave the firm express written permission to call you at other times. Cold callers may call you at work at any time.

Cold Callers Must Say Who's Calling and Why — Cold callers must promptly tell you:

> Their name

> Their firm's name

> Their firm's address or telephone number

> The purpose of the call — for example, to sell you an investment or investment-related services

Caller ID Tip: If you have Caller ID activated on your phone, you should be able to tell when a telemarketer is calling. The Federal Communications Commission requires telemarketers to transmit Caller ID information. Telemarketers may not block their numbers.

Additional Responsibilities of Cold Callers — Cold callers must also:

> **Put you on their "Do Not Call" list, if you ask.** Every securities firm must keep a "do not call" list. If you want to stop sales calls from that firm, tell the caller to put your name and telephone number on the firm's "do not call" list. If anyone from that firm calls you again, get the caller's name and telephone number, note the date and time of the call, and complain to the firm's compliance officer, the SEC, the FINRA, or your state's securities regulator. Further below, you'll find information on how to make a complaint.

Note: Once you're on a firm-specific do-not-call-list, neither the firm nor any of its employees are allowed to call you—even if there is an established business relationship.

> **Treat you with respect.** Cold callers can't threaten, intimidate, or use obscene or profane language. They can't call you repeatedly to annoy, abuse, or harass you.

Get your written approval before taking money directly from your bank accounts. Before investing, you should always get answers to the questions below and written information about the investment. If you do decide to buy from a cold caller, do not give your checking or savings account numbers to the broker over the phone. Brokers *must* get your *written* permission -- such as your signature on a check or an authorization form -- before they can use money from your checking or savings account to fund your investments.

Tell you the truth. People selling securities must tell you the truth. If they don't, brokers violate federal and state securities laws.

What Are Signs of Trouble?

Cold calling is used legitimately to find clients for the long term. These callers ask questions to understand your financial situation and investment goals *before* recommending that you buy anything. Unfortunately, not everyone has your best financial interest at heart. Watch for these signs of trouble:

High-pressure sales tactics. Aggressive cold callers speak from persuasive scripts that include retorts for your every objection. As long as you stay on the phone, they'll keep trying to sell. And they won't let you get a word in edgewise.

Pitches that stress "once-in-a-lifetime" opportunities. Watch out for someone who tells you about a "once-in-a-lifetime" opportunity, especially when the caller bases the recommendation on "inside" or "confidential" information.

Callers touting companies with "breakthrough technologies." These technologies play off of legitimate technologies, but at the same time sound just a little too good to be true.

Callers who refuse to send you written information about the investment. This is a form of manipulation designed to force a quick decision. You should be able to receive information about an investment and take as much time as you need to review it.

Calls from unregistered and unsupervised salespersons. Cold-calling "brokers" and their bosses may not be properly registered to sell securities—and often operate in an environment completely devoid of required supervisory procedures. You can verify whether the caller is registered to sell securities by using FINRA BrokerCheck.

What Else Can You Do?

When cold callers use harassing, abusive sales tactics and lie to you about investment opportunities, they violate the cold calling rules and break federal and state securities laws. Don't let them off the hook!

Report abusive cold callers. You can file a complaint with the SEC, FINRA, your state's securities regulator or the FTC:

U.S. Securities and Exchange Commission

Investors may file a complaint electronically at the SEC Investor Complaint Center or call or fax:
Phone: (800) 732-0330 (toll-free)
Fax: (202) 772-9295

FINRA

Investors may file a complaint electronically at the FINRA Investor Complaint Center or call or fax:
Phone: (240) 386-HELP (4357)
Fax: (866) 397-3290

Your State's Securities Regulator

Investors may file a complaint electronically at the North American Securities Administrators Association (NASAA) Complaint Center or call:
Phone: (888) 846-2722 (toll-free)

Federal Trade Commission

You may file an online complaint at www.donotcall.gov or call:
Phone: (888) 382-1222 (toll-free)

> **Tell intrusive cold callers not to call again.** If you're annoyed by cold callers, stop them before they start their sales pitch. Put your name on the National Do Not Call Registry—and inform the cold caller your name is on the list. Tell the caller to put you on the firm's "do not call" list. If anyone from that firm calls you again, complain to the firm's compliance officer, the SEC, FINRA and your state's securities regulator.

Don't warm up to intrusive cold callers. Cold callers often try to "warm up" potential customers with flattery or friendship. They might try to put you off guard by chatting about your hometown or the local sports team. Or they might suggest they've spoken with you before. Don't fall for their tactics. And don't feel compelled to be polite or stay on the line. You don't have to listen if you don't want to, and you don't have to tell cold callers about yourself or your finances. Say "no, thanks" or "I'm not interested" -- and then hang up. Don't wait for the caller to end the call. YOU are in control and can hang up at any time.

What If I Want to Invest?

Never buy an investment based simply on a telephone sales pitch. A wise investor will always slow down, ask questions, get written information about the investment, and investigate the background of the firm and broker. Take notes so you have a record of what the broker told you, in case you have a dispute later. Before making a final decision and handing over your hard-earned money, take the time to investigate. Follow these steps:

Check out the firm and broker. Use FINRA BrokerCheck to learn about the professional background, registration/license statuses and conduct of FINRA registered firms and their registered brokers.

Call your state's securities regulator. You'll find contact information for your state securities regulator on NASAA's Web site.

Is the investment registered?

Is the broker licensed to do business in my state?

Have you received any complaints about the broker pushing the investment or the broker's firm? Does either have a disciplinary history?

Have you received any complaints about the stock, the company, or the company's managers?

Ask your broker these questions:

Is the investment registered with the SEC and the state securities agency where I live?

How long has the company been in business? Is it making money? If so, how? What is its product or service? Have the people who are managing this company ever made money for investors in the past? Will you send me the latest reports that have been filed on this company? How can I get more information about this investment?

Where does the stock trade? How can I get information about the stock's trading price? How easily can I sell? What price would I get if I decide to sell immediately?

How does this match my investment objectives? What is

the risk that I could lose the money I invest?

What are the costs to buy, hold, and sell this investment?

Do your own research. Get as much written information about the investment as you can. Ask for a prospectus, annual report, offering circular, and financial statements. Commercial Web sites or your local library may have resources that provide additional information about the company, such as lawsuits, liens, or recent credit reports. Compare the written information to what you've been told over the phone. Watch out if you're told that no written information about the company is available. If that happens, contact the SEC, FINRA or your state's securities regulator immediately.

Get a second opinion. Talk to a trusted financial advisor or your attorney. Consider calling another firm for a second opinion on the opportunity.

Monitor your investment. If you decide to invest, watch your investment closely. Make sure your broker sends you account statements and written confirmation of all trades. Read these documents carefully to make sure they are correct. Be alert for any transactions you did not authorize.

Remember, there are rules governing cold calling. It pays to know them — and don't hesitate to take action in the event the caller does not abide by them.

Additional Resources

National Do Not Call Registry

FCC Alert, National Do-Not-Call Registry

Chapter Six

Checking Out Brokers, Advisers and Questions to Ask

a. Check Out Brokers and Investment Advisers
b. Research Investment Advisers.
c. Tips for Checking Out Brokers and Investment Advisers
d. Questions You Should Ask About Your Investments
e. How to Handle Problems

a. Check Out Brokers and Investment Advisers

Research Individual Brokers or Firms.
➤ You can start by visiting //www.finra.org/brokercheck . Check out your broker with BrokerCheck sponsored by FINRA (Financial Industry Regulatory Authority). The agency oversees the people and firms that sell stocks, bonds, mutual funds and other securities. Simply type in your current or prospective broker's name to see employment history, certifications, and licenses—as well as regulatory actions, violations or complaints you might want to know about.

You also can get information about your broker's firm. There's no reason not to check.

b. Research Investment Advisers. You can start by visiting http://www.adviserinfo.sec.gov/IAPD/Content/IapdMain/iapd_SiteMap.aspx . On this website you can **search for an Investment Adviser firm** and view the registration or reporting form ("Form ADV") that the adviser filed. This website will also search **FINRA's BrokerCheck system** and indicate whether an entity is a Brokerage firm. Investment advisers file Form ADV to register with the SEC and/or the states. Some advisers that do not have to register with the SEC or the states ("Exempt Reporting Advisers") must nonetheless complete some of the questions in Form ADV for purposes of reporting to the SEC and/or the states. Form ADV contains information about an investment adviser and its business operations. Additionally, it contains disclosure about certain disciplinary events involving the adviser and its key personnel.

You can also **search for an individual investment adviser representative** and view that individual's professional background and conduct, including current registrations, employment history, and disclosures about certain disciplinary events involving the individual. The information

about investment adviser representatives
that appears on this website is collected
from individual Investment Adviser
Representatives, Investment Adviser firm(s),
and/or securities regulator(s) as part of the
securities industry's registration and
licensing process. Individuals that are
Registered Representatives of a Brokerage
firm that are listed in **FINRA's
BrokerCheck system** will also appear in
search results.

**If you have technical difficulties using
the Investment Adviser Public
Disclosure site?**
You can call 240-386-4848 for technical
assistance.

c. Tips for Checking Out Brokers and Investment Advisers

Federal or state securities laws require
brokers, investment advisers, and their firms
to be licensed or registered, and to make
important information public. But it's up to you
to find that information and use it to protect
your investment dollars. The good news is that
this information is easy to get, and one phone
call or web search may save you from sending
your money to a con artist, an unscrupulous
financial professional, or a disreputable firm.

Before you invest or pay for any investment advice, make sure your brokers, investment advisers, and investment adviser representatives have not had disciplinary problems or been in trouble with regulators or other investors. You also should check to see whether they are registered or licensed.

This is very important, because if you do business with an unregistered securities broker or a firm that later goes out of business, there may be no way for you to recover your money — even if an arbitrator or a court rules in your favor.

Brokers and Brokerage Firms

The Central Registration Depository (CRD) is a computerized database that contains information about most brokers, their representatives, and the firms they work for. For instance, you can find out if brokers are properly licensed in your state and if they have had disciplinary problems with regulators or received serious complaints from investors. You'll also find information about the brokers' educational backgrounds and where they've worked before their current jobs.

You can ask your state securities regulator or the Financial Industry Regulatory Authority (FINRA) to provide you with information from the CRD. Because your state securities regulator may provide more comprehensive information from the CRD than FINRA, especially when it comes to investor complaints, you may want to check with your state securities regulator first. You'll find contact information for your state securities regulator on the website of the North American Securities Administrators Association. To contact FINRA, either visit FINRA's BrokerCheck website or call FINRA's toll-free BrokerCheck hotline at (800) 289-9999.

Investment Advisers

People or firms that get paid to give advice about investing in securities generally must register with either the SEC or the state securities agency where they have their principal place of business. As discussed in greater detail below, the rules governing the registration of certain investment advisers have changed.

On July 21, 2010, the Dodd-Frank Wall Street Reform and Consumer Protection Act ("Dodd-Frank Act") was signed into law. The Dodd-Frank Act amends certain provisions of the Investment Advisers Act of 1940 by delegating generally to the states responsibility over certain mid-sized investment advisers – *i.e.*, those that have between $25 million and $100 million of assets under management ("AUM").

The Dodd-Frank Act and SEC rules increased the threshold above which all investment advisers must register with the SEC from $30 million to $110 million of AUM. Prior to July 2011, an investment adviser regulated by the state in which it maintained its principal office and place of business generally was prohibited from registering with the SEC unless the adviser had at least $25 million of AUM, and was required to register with the SEC once it had at least $30 million of AUM. Now, investment advisers with less than $110 million of AUM may be prohibited from registering with the SEC, depending on the size of the adviser's AUM and whether the adviser meets other requirements.

This means that state securities authorities will have primary regulatory authority over a substantial number of investment advisers that previously were subject to primary regulation by the SEC. Larger investment advisers, generally, those with over $100 million of AUM, will continue to be registered with the SEC and will be subject to federal regulation (state investment adviser laws requiring registration, licensing, and qualification have been preempted for these advisers).

Some investment advisers employ investment adviser representatives, the people who actually work with clients. In most cases, these people must be licensed or registered with your state securities regulator to do business with you. So be sure to check them out with your state securities regulator.

To find out about an investment adviser and whether it is properly registered, read its registration form, called "Form ADV." Form ADV has two parts. Part 1 contains information about the adviser's business and whether the adviser has had problems with regulators or clients. Part 2 sets out the minimum requirements for a written disclosure statement, commonly referred to as the "brochure," which advisers must provide to prospective clients initially and to existing clients annually. The brochure describes, in a narrative format, the adviser's business practices, fees, conflicts of interest, and disciplinary information. Before you hire an investment adviser, always ask for and carefully read both parts of the Form ADV.

Where applicable, each brochure provided to clients must be accompanied by a "brochure supplement" that includes information about the specific individuals, acting on behalf of the adviser, who actually provide investment advice and interact with the client. An adviser must deliver the brochure supplement to the client before or at the time that the specific individual begins to provide investment advice to the client.

You can view an adviser's most recent Form ADV online by visiting the Investment Adviser Public Disclosure (IAPD) website. You can also obtain copies of Form ADV for individual advisers and firms from the investment adviser, your state securities regulator, or the SEC, depending on the size of the adviser. You'll find contact information for your state securities regulator on the website of the North American Securities Administrators Association.

If the investment adviser is registered with the SEC, you can get a copy of Form ADV (Part 1 only) by accessing information on "How to Request Public Documents" at http://www.sec.gov/answers/publicdocs.htm. In addition, at the SEC's headquarters, you can visit our Public Reference Room from 10:00 a.m. to 3:00 p.m. to obtain copies of SEC records and documents.

Because some investment advisers and their representatives are also brokers, you may want to check both BrokerCheck and Form ADV.

Conclusion

Once you've checked out the registration and record of your financial professional or firm, there's more to do. For example, if you plan to do business with a brokerage firm, you should find out whether the brokerage firm and its clearing firm are members of the Securities Investor Protection Corporation (SIPC). SIPC provides limited customer protection if a brokerage firm becomes insolvent — although it **does not** insure against losses attributable to a decline in the market value of your securities. If you've placed your cash or securities in the hands of a non-SIPC member, you may not be eligible for SIPC coverage if the firm goes out of business.

Here are a few questions to get you started.

What experience do you have, especially with people in my circumstances?
Where did you go to school? What is your recent employment history?
What licenses do you hold? Are you registered with the SEC, a state, or FINRA?
Are the firm, the clearing firm, and any other related companies that will do business with me members of SIPC?
What products and services do you offer? Can you recommend only a limited number of products or services to me? If so, why?
How are you paid for your services? What is your usual hourly rate, flat fee, or commission?
Have you ever been disciplined by any government regulator for unethical or improper conduct or been sued by a client who was not happy with the work you did?
For registered investment advisers, will you send me a copy of both parts of your Form ADV?

For more questions and additional tips, be sure to read our publications, Ask Questions and Get the Facts on Saving and Investing. In addition, although the SEC cannot recommend or endorse any particular entity, there are a number of non-profit educational and consumer organizations that offer free tools to help investors check financial professionals. For example, AARP offers a Financial Adviser Questionnaire, and the Certified Financial Planner Board of Standards has a Checklist for Interviewing a Financial Planner.

http://www.sec.gov/investor/brokers.htm [xli]

d. Questions You Should Ask About Your Investments

That's the best advice we can give you about how to invest wisely. We see too many investors who might have avoided trouble and losses if they had asked basic questions from the start.

We encourage you to thoroughly evaluate the background of any financial professional with whom you intend to do business—*before* you hand over your hard-earned cash.

Investor Tip

Which financial professional you select is very important for several reasons. You'll want to investigate thoroughly before doing business with a financial professional or firm that has a history of complaints or problems with regulators. Also, you should know that if your financial professional or his or her firm goes out of business or declares bankruptcy, you might not be able to recover your money—even if an arbitrator or a court rules in your favor.

It doesn't matter if you are a beginner or have been investing for many years, it's never too early or too late to start asking questions. It's almost impossible to ask a dumb question about how you are investing your money. Don't feel intimidated. Remember, it's your money at stake. You are paying for the assistance of a financial professional.

A good financial professional will welcome your questions, no matter how basic. Financial professionals know that an educated client is an asset, not a liability. They would rather answer your questions before you invest, than confront your anger and confusion later.

In this brochure, you'll find some questions that you should ask about investment products, the people who sell those products, and the people who provide investment advice to you. We've also included some tips on how to monitor your investments and handle any problems.

Keep this brochure on hand when considering an investment and use it by asking the right questions before you buy. Have a pen and piece of paper ready to take notes on the answers. They can come in handy if there is a dispute later about what was said during the transaction. Taking notes also sends a signal to your financial professional: I'm a smart and serious investor who wants to know more about the risks and rewards of investing.

Questions About Products:

> Is this investment product registered with the SEC and my state securities agency?
> Does this investment match my investment goals? Why is this investment suitable for me?

How will this investment make money? (Dividends? Interest? Capital gains?) Specifically, what must happen for this investment to increase in value? (For example, increase in interest rates, real estate values, or market share?)

What are the total fees to purchase, maintain, and sell this investment? Are there ways that I can reduce or avoid some of the fees that I'll pay, such as purchasing the investment directly? After all the fees are paid, how much does this investment have to increase in value before I break even?

How liquid is this investment? How easy would it be to sell if I needed my money right away?

What are the specific risks associated with this investment? What is the maximum I could lose? (For example, what will be the effect of changing interest rates, economic recession, high competition, or stock market ups and downs?)

How long has the company been in business? Is its management experienced? Has management been successful in the past? Have they ever made money for investors before?

Is the company making money? How are they doing compared to their competitors?

Where can I get more information about this investment? Can I get the latest reports filed by the company with the SEC: a prospectus or offering circular, or the latest annual report and financial statements?

For mutual funds:

How has this fund performed over the long run? Where can I get an independent evaluation of this fund? What specific risks are associated with this fund?
What type of securities does the fund hold? How often does the portfolio change?
Does this mutual fund invest in any type of securities that could cause the value to go up or down rapidly in a short period of time? (For example, derivatives?)
How does the fund perform compared to other funds of the same type or to an index of the same type of investment?
How much will the fund charge me when I buy shares? What ongoing fees are charged? How much will the fund charge me when I sell shares?
Is the fund portable? If I move my assets to another firm, will I be able to continue holding the fund or will I need to liquidate it?

Questions About The People Who Sell Investments or Provide Investment Advice:

Are you registered with our state securities regulator? Have you ever been disciplined by the SEC, a state regulator, or other organization (such as NASD or one of the stock exchanges)?

Investor Tip - Check Out Your Financial Professional

You can verify your broker's disciplinary history by checking the Central Registration Depository (CRD). Either your state securities regulator or NASD can provide you with CRD information. Your state securities regulator may give you more information from the CRD than NASD, especially when it comes to investor complaints, so you may want to check with them first. You'll find contact information for your state securities regulator on the website of the North American Securities Administrators Association. To contact FINRA, visit FINRA's BrokerCheck website, or call them toll-free at (800)289-9999.

You can find out about investment advisers and whether they are properly registered by reading their registration forms, called the "Form ADV." You can view an adviser's most recent Form ADV online by visiting the Investment Adviser Public Disclosure (IAPD) website. At present, the IAPD database contains Forms ADV only for investment adviser firms that register electronically using the Investment Adviser Registration Depository. You can also get copies of Form ADV for individual advisers and firms from the investment adviser, your state securities regulator, or the SEC, depending on the size of the adviser.

How long has your firm been in business? How many arbitration awards have been filed against your firm?
What training and experience do you have? How long have you been in the business? What other firms have you been registered with? What is the status of those firms today?
Have you personally been involved in any arbitration cases? What happened?
What is your investment philosophy?

Describe your typical client. Can you provide me with some names and telephone numbers of your long term clients?

How do you get paid? By commission? Amount of assets you manage? Another method?

Do I have any choices on how to pay you?
 Should I pay you by the transaction? Or a flat fee regardless of how many transactions I have?

Do you make more if I buy this stock (or bond, or mutual fund) rather than another?
If you weren't making extra money, would your recommendation be the same?

Are you participating in a sales contest?

Is this purchase really in my best interest, or are you trying to win a prize?

You've told me what it costs me to buy this stock (or bond, or mutual fund); how much will I receive if I sell it today?

Where do you send my order to be executed?

Can we get a better price if we send it to another market?

If your financial professional changes firms, ask: Did they pay you to change firms?
Do you get anything for bringing me along?

Questions About the Progress of Your Investments:

How frequently do I get statements?

Do I understand what the statement tells me?

Is the return on my investment meeting my expectations and goals?

Is this investment performing as I was led to believe?

How much money will I get back if I sell my investment today?

How much am I paying in commission or fees?

Have my goals changed? If so, are my investments still suitable?

What criteria will I use to decide when to sell?

e. How to Handle Problems:

Act promptly! By law, you only have a limited time to take legal action. Follow these steps to solve your problem:

1. Talk to your financial professional and explain the problem. Where is the fault? Were communications clear? Refer to your notes. What did the financial professional tell you? What do your notes say?
2. If your financial professional can't resolve your problem, then talk to the financial professional's supervisor (which, for brokers, is often the firm's branch manager).
3. If the problem is still not resolved, write to the compliance department at the firm's main office. Explain your problem clearly, and how you want it resolved. Ask the compliance office to respond to you within 30 days. If you're still not satisfied:
4. Send us your complaint by using our online complaint form or you can reach us as follows:

> Securities and Exchange Commission
> Office of Investor Education and Advocacy
> 100 F Street, N.E.
> Washington, D.C. 20549-0213

At the SEC, we will research your complaint, contact the firm or person you have complained about and ask them to respond to your specific complaint or question. Sometimes our intervention yields a satisfactory result. If these steps don't work, you may need to take legal action on your own. We can send you information on mediation and arbitration, and suggest how to locate a lawyer if you need one.

Investor Tip

When you ask these questions, write down the answers you receive and what you decided to do. If something goes wrong, your notes can help to establish what was said. Let your financial professional know you're taking notes. They'll know you're a serious investor and may tell you more. Use our form for taking notes when you speak to your financial professional.

For more information on how to invest wisely, ask for the following Security and Exchange publications:
Invest Wisely: Advice From Your Securities Industry Regulators, Protect Your Money: Check Out Brokers and Investment Advisers,

and Invest Wisely: An Introduction to Mutual Funds. You can also get other SEC publications online or by calling our toll-free publications line at (800) SEC-0330.

http://www.sec.gov/investor/pubs/askquestions.htm [xlii]

Book Review

Thank you for reading my book Basic Understanding of Bond Investments Book Five - for Teens and Young Adults. Please, if you liked the book take a spare moment as it would be a great help if you could post a review of it on Amazon and let other potential readers know why you liked it. It's not necessary to write a lengthy, formal review—a summary of the comments from you would be perfectly fine.

About the Author

Ronald E. Hudkins (1951-Present) now residing in Durango, Colorado was born in Canton, Ohio and raised in Massillon, Ohio. He was drafted into military service in 1970 where he remained up until 1993 when he retired honorably from the U.S. Army, Military Police Corps. During his service, after and in between a lot of traveling he attended many universities that include Kent State

University, Maryland University, Central Texas College (European Branch), Blair Junior College, Hagerstown Junior College and Phoenix University. He

*The Author
Ronald E. Hudkins*

declared two majors in the areas of Business Administration and a Bachelor of Science in Information Technology.

Ronald has been writing as a hobby for over twenty years. He has completed a collection of multiple genres in both fiction and nonfiction that include financial, estate, cooking and identity theft. In the area of fiction he has published humor, science fiction and fantasy. He is polishing up some children's, paranormal romance, romance and additional science fiction books. He has approximately 50 additional plot outlines completed and their associated books in various stages of completion. We can anticipate more stories in the areas of finance, children's and young adult reading as well as humor, fantasy, romance, thrillers and even some mystery and steampunk. Only the author's files and mind know the definitive creations yet to be.

He is a Platinum Level Expert author at http://ezinearticles.com/expert=Ronald_Hudkins where he has published over 100 articles in 29 separate niches which have amassed over 74,000 views.

He participates on social sites, such as Facebook and Twitter, videos on YouTube and slid presentations too many and numerous to list. Needless to say, he stays occupied and busy and as such - we all benefit. See his other projects page on his author website at: http://www.ronaldhudkins.com

Author's Other Books

Listed at www.RonaldHudkins.com

Fiction Categories

Children's Books

Two Different Pictures (Activity Book), Book 16, Published August 28, 2014

The World Outside (Adventure), Book 17, Published September 16, 2014

Fantasy

The Cape Coral Heroes, Book 9, Published March 19, 2014

Humor

Senior Things I Said, Say, Did and Do, Book 3 published December 21, 2013

The Summer of Lost Soles, Book 4, published March 20, 2013

Science Fiction

The Thirty Century War, Book 5, published November 16, 2013

Paranormal Romance (Teen)

The River of Love – Surfacing, Book 7, Published (April 11, 2015)

Romance (Erotica Adult)

Stay the Night, Book 10, Published May 10, 2014

Longing Love and Coming Home, Book 15, Published August 24, 2014

Steampunk

The First Steampunk Adventures – Tales One thru Five, Book 22, Published May 21, 2015

The Second Steampunk Adventures – Tales Six thru 10, Book 23, projected June 2015

Nonfiction Categories

Computer References

Your Digital Footprint – Password Protection Requirements, Book 11, Published June 12, 2014

Cookbooks

What Makes Cannabis Recipes Work, Book 6, Published December 26, 2013

100 Easy Holiday Platters for New Year's, Book 18, Published January 20, 2015

Financial References (Teen and Young Adult)

Basic Savings and Checking Account Maintenance – Book One for Teens and Young Adults, Book 8, Published March 7, 2014

Basic Budget Establishment and Maintenance – Book Two for Teens and Young Adults, Book 19, Published February Four, 2015

Understanding Penny Stock Market – Book Three for Teens and Young Adults, Book 12, Published August 22, 2014

Basic Understanding of the Stock Market – Book Four for Teens and Young Adults, Book 20, Published February 8, 2015

Basic Understanding of Bond Investments – Book Five for Teens and Young Adults, Book 21, Published February 22, 2015

Basic Understanding of Financial Investment – Book Six for Teens and Young Adults, Book 24, Published June 22, 2015

Self Help

Asset Protection and Estate Planning for All Ages, Book 1, Published July 12, 2007

How to Avoid Identity Theft, Book 2, Published June 15, 2011

Medical References

Lower Your High Blood Pressure Naturally Without a Prescription, Book 14, Published October 27, 2014

Pet References

45 Foods that Kill Your Dog and 21 Other Things, Book 13, Published August 12, 2014

Additional Books are likely published. To see or obtain any of this author's publications visit the Authors' Writing Platform @ www.RonaldHudkins.com

Thank You for the Visit !!!

References

[i] http://investor.gov/introduction-markets/why-invest
[ii] http://investor.gov/investing-basics/guiding-principles/five-questions-ask-before-you-invest
[iii] http://investor.gov/researching-managing-investments/investing-your-own/direct-investing
[iv] http://investor.gov/investing-basics/investment-products
[v] http://investor.gov/investing-basics/investment-products/saving-your-childs-education-529-plans
[vi] http://investor.gov/investing-basics/investment-products/annuities
[vii] http://investor.gov/investing-basics/investment-products/bonds
[viii] http://investor.gov/investing-basics/investment-products/certificates-deposit-cds
[ix] http://investor.gov/investing-basics/investment-products/commodities
[x] http://investor.gov/investing-basics/investment-products/corporate-bonds
[xi] http://investor.gov/investing-basics/investment-products/exchange-traded-funds-etfs
[xii] http://investor.gov/investing-basics/investment-products/hedge-funds
[xiii] http://investor.gov/investing-basics/investment-products/high-yield-corporate-bonds
[xiv] http://investor.gov/investing-basics/investment-products/international-investing
[xv] http://investor.gov/investing-basics/investment-products/municipal-bonds
[xvi] http://investor.gov/investing-basics/investment-products/mutual-funds
[xvii] http://investor.gov/investing-basics/investment-products/real-estate-investment-trusts-reits
[xviii] http://investor.gov/investing-basics/investment-products/savings-bonds
[xix] http://investor.gov/investing-basics/investment-products/stocks
[xx] http://investor.gov/investing-basics/investment-products/structured-notes-principal-protection
[xxi] http://investor.gov/investing-basics/investment-products/target-date-funds

[xxii] http://investor.gov/news-alerts/investor-bulletins/investor-bulletin-variable-annuities-introduction

[xxiii] http://investor.gov/investing-basics/guiding-principles/asset-allocation

[xxiv] http://investor.gov/investing-basics/guiding-principles/what-is-risk

[xxv] http://investor.gov/investing-basics/guiding-principles/assessing-your-risk-tolerance

[xxvi] http://investor.gov/investing-basics/avoiding-fraud

[xxvii] http://investor.gov/investing-basics/avoiding-fraud/what-you-can-do-avoid-investment-fraud

[xxviii] http://investor.gov/investing-basics/avoiding-fraud/protect-your-social-media-accounts

[xxix] http://investor.gov/investing-basics/avoiding-fraud/types-fraud/affinity-fraud

[xxx] http://investor.gov/investing-basics/avoiding-fraud/types-fraud/high-yield-investment-programs

[xxxi] http://investor.gov/investing-basics/avoiding-fraud/types-fraud/internet-social-media-fraud

[xxxii] http://investor.gov/investing-basics/avoiding-fraud/types-fraud/ponzi-scheme

[xxxiii] http://investor.gov/investing-basics/avoiding-fraud/types-fraud/pre-ipo-investment-scams

[xxxiv] http://investor.gov/investing-basics/avoiding-fraud/types-fraud/pyramid-scheme

[xxxv] http://investor.gov/investing-basics/avoiding-fraud/types-fraud/prime-bank-investments

[xxxvi] http://investor.gov/investing-basics/avoiding-fraud/types-fraud/promissory-notes

[xxxvii] http://investor.gov/investing-basics/avoiding-fraud/types-fraud/pump-dump-schemes

[xxxviii]

http://www.cftc.gov/ConsumerProtection/FraudAwarenessPrevention/CFTCFraudAdvisories/fraudadv_commoditypool

[xxxix]

http://www.cftc.gov/ConsumerProtection/FraudAwarenessPrevention/CFTCFraudAdvisories/fraudadv_forex

[xl]

http://www.cftc.gov/ConsumerProtection/FraudAwarenessPrevention/CFTCFraudAdvisories/fraudadv_preciousmetals

[xli] http://www.sec.gov/investor/brokers.htm

[xlii] http://www.sec.gov/investor/pubs/askquestions.htm

www.ingramcontent.com/pod-product-compliance
Lightning Source LLC
Chambersburg PA
CBHW051901170526
45168CB00001B/192